Village '
in
WEST SUSSEX

Douglas Lasseter

COUNTRYSIDE BOOKS
NEWBURY, BERKSHIRE

COUNTRYSIDE BOOKS
3 Catherine Road
Newbury, Berkshire

ISBN 1 85306 455 6

The picture on page 88 showing the Priest House, West Hoathly, is
with the kind permission of the Sussex Archaeological Society.

Designed by Graham Whiteman
Front cover photograph shows West Chiltington village.

Maps by the author
Photographs by Eileen Lasseter

Produced through MRM Associates Ltd., Reading
Printed by Woolnough Bookbinding Ltd., Irthlingborough

Contents

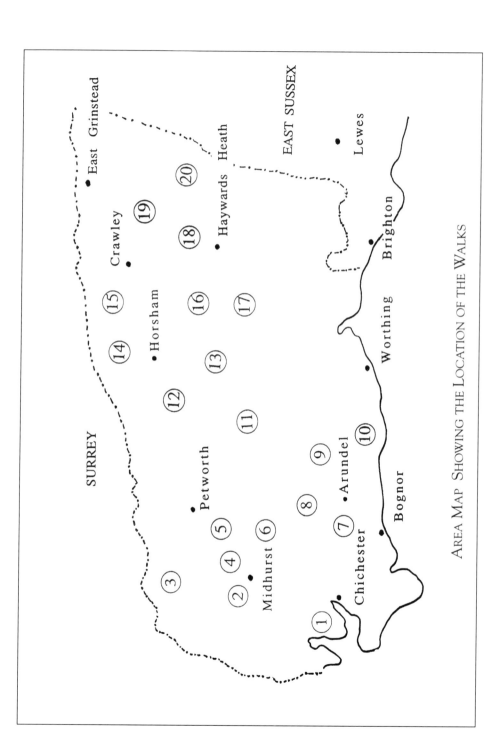

AREA MAP SHOWING THE LOCATION OF THE WALKS

WALK

⋘⋙

*My thanks yet again to Eileen and Susan for all their hard work
and the support of the Sussex Wayfarers Walking Group.
But especially to Philip Jones who, against the odds,
is still out there, walking and watching, in our countryside!*

Publisher's Note

We hope that you obtain considerable enjoyment from this book; great care has been taken in its preparation. Although at the time of publication all routes followed public rights of way or permitted paths, diversion orders can be made and permissions withdrawn.

We cannot of course be held responsible for such diversion orders and any inaccuracies in the text which result from these or any other changes to the routes nor any damage which might result from walkers trespassing on private property. We are anxious though that all details covering the walks are kept up to date and would therefore welcome information from readers which would be relevant to future editions.

Introduction

It is quite surprising from just how far away one can recognise one's own books being carried by fellow walkers journeying to discover their countryside heritage! So, encouraged by this and spurred on by my wife Eileen (loyally supportive and camera happy) and our daughter and her family, I embarked upon this, my third, publication, in the hope that others can be tempted to undertake still more journeys of discovery . . .

In this book, the walks are centred around West Sussex villages, some combined because their geographical location makes it impossible to separate them. All, as you will discover, have hidden treasures that can only be searched out on foot and they range from one which has a Buddhist monastery (to which the general public is invited and where tea can be taken at the appropriate time) to another where the village pub has a grave headstone in the front garden, a sad reminder of the deeply unforgiving prejudices of the last century.

The walks take the reader around each village and the points of interest are highlighted. There is, of course, a pub in each and/or other catering establishments and these are briefly described – but I hasten to add that this is not a food and drink guide. . .one man's meat etc! The routes are circular and vary in distance from 1½ to 7¼ miles. Basic directions are given to enable the reader to reach the various start locations. In addition, each chapter has its own sketch map of both the village and its walk route, together with the Ordnance Survey sheet names for the Landranger (1:50 000) and Pathfinder (1:25 000) series of maps, which hopefully might encourage our readers to explore deeper into each area and the horizons beyond. On that aspect, I come to the question of suitable footwear – when walking beyond the confines of the respective villages sandals and the like should not be worn. Great outlay on boots is not necessary, however; stout trainers are generally satisfactory.

I have indicated places where your car can be left while you walk, but must stress that this should be done with discretion as haphazard parking can easily cause obstruction and friction in small villages. In addition, many of the pub landlords are willing to accommodate walkers' cars, providing they intend to patronise the establishment either before or after their walk, which is entirely reasonable. If in doubt, it's best to ask.

We know you will find areas within these walks and villages and their surroundings which are unbelievably beautiful and, please, when you leave, take only yourselves and your possessions with you so that, with the possible exception of your footprints, you leave no trace of your presence.

We hope that you enjoy these walks as much as we have enjoyed compiling them for you.

Douglas Lasseter

WALK 1

BOSHAM

Length : 1¾ or 3 miles

Getting there: From the A259 (the old route of the A27 trunk road) at Broadbridge roundabout, between Chichester and Nutbourne, turn south into Delling Lane, signposted to Bosham.

Parking: You can use the car park at the Berkeley Arms while you walk (if you also visit the pub). An alternative is the large public car park – very busy at weekends in summer – in the centre of the village.

Despite the fact that it is free, you are strongly advised NOT to park on Shore Road (that is, along the stretch of shoreline south of the village which is exposed at low tide) – Bosham has one of the fastest rise and fall rates of tide on the south coast.

Maps: OS Landranger 197, Chichester and The Downs; Pathfinder, Chichester and Bognor. Starting point GR: 820044.

Bosham is, perhaps, the most historically important place in the South of England and figured large in the Roman scheme of things. It had everything to suit their pur-poses; easy approach and exit on fast rising and falling tides, totally sheltered, large areas which dried out, facilitating the unloading and loading of their vessels, and

FOOD and DRINK

There are two pubs actually in Bosham, the Berkeley Arms, chosen as best suited for our purpose, and the Anchor Bleu, which is sited right on the waterfront. In addition there is a coffee shop/tea room in the High Street.

The Berkeley Arms is situated at the corner junction of Delling and Bosham Lanes and was built about 1790 as a private dwelling place. Bought and converted to a pub at about the turn of this century, it is very comfortable and welcoming, promising 'good ale, good food and good conversation'. It has a wide range of specials, often fish, as well as bar, restaurant and children's menus. There is a small garden. Telephone: 01243 573167.

unhindered access into the immediate area and the hinterland. It was equally important to the Saxons and, indeed, those before them for these very same reasons. It is thought to be the place where Canute (AD 994–1035) attempted his tide-stemming feat. It has been established that he had a palace here and it is now accepted that one of his daughters is buried in the crypt of the church.

Bosham's church is an unbelievably beautiful building which warrants a visit in its own right and is not the place for a quick in/out tourist call. One curious architectural feature that I cannot find an explanation for is that it is not symmetrical about its centre line, for example the chancel is offset to the nave by well over 3 ft.

This was once a major boat building centre but that activity has now sadly diminished. The large agricultural industry, however, continues to thrive on the extensive alluvial plain. The village itself is now supported almost entirely by the tourist trade.

The walk has been deliberately planned around low tide and so is really a shoreline route and it is quite essential that you determine the time of low water. All the local papers carry this information, but if you are travelling from outside the region, you should telephone the Harbour Master's office in West Itchenor (01243 512301).

Bosham is a much written about, sketched, painted and filmed village – the three latter categories almost exclusively at high water, which certainly enhances the beauty and charm of the place. But you will find hidden corners of it which are only accessible at low water, the time most favoured by bird watchers as all areas of Bosham and Chichester Harbours are a major staging post for migrating wildfowl and waders in spring and autumn coming to rest and feed.

The shorter circuit includes the beachside path, the quay and the church, while the longer route allows you to take in estuary views to the south of the village.

THE WALK

❶ From the pub walk west on Bosham Lane, turning right out of the pub. At Critchfield Road, cross over to the opposite pavement, coming then to the Mill Stream Hotel and Restaurant. What

PLACES of INTEREST

Fishbourne Roman Palace is just off the A259 east of Bosham. The excavated buildings are under cover but work is ongoing and exciting discoveries are frequently made. Open all year round.

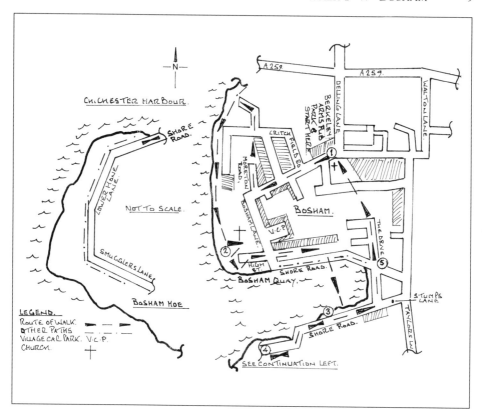

lovely buildings, but note also the charming old thatched cottage on the corner opposite. Here cross over into Moreton Road.

If you are parked in the village centre, simply walk out into Bosham Lane, turn right and walk up to this point.

With the western aspect of the hotel on the right, continue ahead and, with Moreton Road bearing sharply right, walk into the signposted footpath. Coming next to a four-way sign, walk through the gap in the hedge. Next, and with Windmill House facing you, turn right at the two-way sign into an enclosed path. This will bring you to a three-way sign at a stile.

Turn left onto the east bankside path of Chichester Harbour. Going then across a private boat slipway, the path continues along the beach. With two waysigns on the left, turn left then sharply right onto the beachside path. This brings into view the full expanse of the harbour. The right of way now goes into the area of an old boatyard – note the request to keep dogs on leads. You will be heading towards a three-way sign. Using the concrete steps go down onto the beach. Here the steeple of Bosham church will come into view on the left. Then at a slipway and some of the buildings on Bosham Quay, turn left into the signposted path and follow this stony

Bosham harbour

track which brings you to a metalled lane where, in just a few yards, you turn left into an obvious footpath going across Bosham Meadow.

❷ This leads to a footbridge across Bosham Stream and on the other side is the gate into the churchyard. You will see that I have not exaggerated about the church. Leave the churchyard by its east gate and turn sharp right. This will bring you to another footbridge over Bosham Stream and, with Bosham Meadow on your right, turn left, following the direction of the metalled lane. The lane will bring you out very shortly onto the Bosham Quay and once again you will be going over Bosham Stream and will see, to

your left, the old mill building (the quay, its buildings and the meadow are National Trust property). Now on Shore Road, turn left up by the Anchor Bleu pub, then right into High Street where, at the end, you cross over Bosham Lane. If you wish to return to the village car park from here, simply turn left to find it a short distance along on the right. If you are continuing, walk into the twitten. This elevated path will take you by the frontages of some of old Bosham's cottages and houses, which, in their day, would have housed the ship-yard workers. (If you were so minded you could have continued along Shore Road, of course.)

Coming to a set of steps, go down them and turn right on the causeway path going across the harbour. At low tide it is totally dry and safe. Once over on the other part of Shore Road you again have a choice. If you have opted for the shorter walk, you can return to a) the public car park by turning left and continuing along Shore Road to go right into Bosham Lane, or b) the Berkeley Arms by also turning left but then walking into The Drive and following the directions in point 5 below. If, however, you want to do the full walk, turn right.

❸ Continuing west along Shore Road, you pass a waysign on the left (you will use this path on your return). Passing by Silvermere, continue. Just beyond a group of houses, bear left onto a gravelled footpath elevated above the road. You may well want to take advantage of the seats in various places along this route to enjoy the lovely views of Old Bosham across the harbour. Eventually you will have to use Shore Road again, then just before rounding a corner in the road, bear right onto a clearly defined path which cuts the corner off. Coming out onto the road again, cross it and at the waysign, go through a wicket gate, turning right into a garden. The houses will be on your left. Now, with a hedge on your right, the grassy track will take you out onto field paths. The hedge still on your right, a two-way sign will direct you back onto Shore Road. Another waysign here points in the direction of the

harbour beach and if you feel adventurous then by all means continue the walk which eventually goes all the way round to Bosham Hoe, from where you can return on the road. If you do so, be mindful of the tidal state, and, of course, this adds further mileage to the walk.

❹ However, you may now use the whole length of Shore Road to wander back from this point. You will come to the place where you turned off through the wicket gate and here, no doubt, you will see the advantage of cutting across the grass to avoid the bend in the road. Then, just beyond Silvermere, on your right now, bear right into the waysigned path. With Creek Cottage on the left, it will continue by the backs of the other old cottages and houses along its length. Coming to a garage on the right, bear right onto its driveway to come out onto the junction of Shore Road, The Drive and Stumps Lane.

❺ Now, at this point, I refer those of you who are parked in the village to the directions in 2a) above. For those parking at the pub, walk ahead into The Drive and at its top continue on into the twitten. You will pass, on your left, a cemetery – shortly beyond cross over a concrete road and go into the opposite twitten. There at the end of its short length, you will come out opposite the Berkeley Arms.

TROTTON AND CHITHURST

Length : 4¼ miles

Getting there: Trotton is a widely dispersed village. This walk starts from its pub, directly off the A272. Travelling west on the A272 from Midhurst, pass the sign to Chithurst and take the turning signposted left to Dumpford around the next bend. The Keepers Arms is immediately on your left. Travelling east on the A272, cross Trotton Bridge (controlled by traffic lights) and the turning to Dumpford and the Keepers Arms is the next on the right. Care is needed when turning off the A272 here, from either direction.

Parking: Permission to leave your car at the Keepers Arms while you walk is readily given, with the usual proviso. You should not attempt to park in Terwick Lane (leading to Dumpford).

Maps: OS Landranger 197, Chichester and The Downs; Pathfinder, Midhurst and Petworth. Starting point GR: 838222.

This is a thoroughly rural walk, taking in these two ancient villages, both of which, because of their manorial status, were cov-ered in the Domesday Census. The first section of the walk goes across sandy Trotton Common. You then go northwards to

FOOD and DRINK

Trotton's one pub, the Keepers Arms, is the only such establishment for some way around. It is open six days a week, Tuesday through to Sunday, with a limited choice of food on Sunday evenings. There are interesting specials, including fondues, and wherever possible fresh ingredients are used. The management are 'dog and children friendly' albeit during daylight hours only. There are tables outside the pub, but no garden. Telephone: 01730 813521.

Chithurst, as compact a community as Trotton is scattered, and when crossing the river Rother you will catch the first glimpse of the hub of this village, its small and beautiful church and almost adjoining manor house.

A near neighbour of the manor is Chithurst House, now a Buddhist monastery, Cittaviveka, which provides religious instruction and teaching for both monks and nuns, and is a centre for meditation and retreat. Visitors are welcome here in the afternoon, to the building's ground floor and gardens, with the proviso that footwear must be removed and clothing must cover the upper arms and legs. Tea is offered at 5.30 pm. Telephone: 01730 814986. There is a car park here which you can use if you decide to complete the walk and visit the monastery later.

The route continues into the country to the west and connects with an ancient track, Brier Lane, probably an old drove road. Then, via other paths, you come to the south side of Trotton village, with an opportunity to visit the parish church, St George's, and what a lovely old building it is, with its well-preserved wall murals.

THE WALK

❶ Leave the pub and, with Love Hill Farm opposite, turn left onto Terwick Lane. Then at the entrance to Spring Cottage and a two-way sign, both on the left, bear left into a track going off the lane and almost at once pass another two-way sign, also on the left. Bearing into the left-hand fork and just beyond, pass by Love Hill and Steedles Cottages on the right. The sandy track will soon take you up another level onto Trotton Common and, with a three-way sign on your right, turn left into (at first) a wide sandy and grass track. With a two-way sign on the left, take the right-hand fork. Descend to the A272 and cross straight into the opposite junction, Chithurst Lane, with a wood sculpture and art studio on your right. As you continue up the lane you pass a waysign on the left, then Whites Farm and three old cottages also on your left. Thus far you have still been in Trotton but beyond its boundary sign on the right you are in Chithurst and soon to be on its bridge over the river Rother, with your first glimpse of St Mary's, its parish church.

If you want to visit the monastery, continue up Chithurst Lane to find it on your left, shortly beyond the church and the

PLACES of INTEREST

To the south-west of Trotton is **South Harting**, such a picturesque place with a lovely old church. A great many of its buildings are constructed with a particular type of hard chalk called clunch which mellows to a beautifully warm cream colour. **Uppark House** (NT), recently reopened after being almost totally gutted by fire, is just to the south of the village on the B2141.

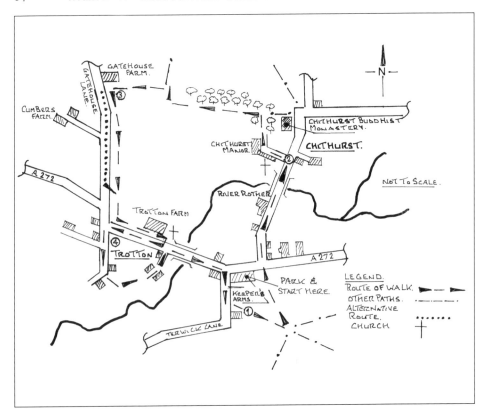

manor house. Afterwards you can either return to the church and continue the walk, as below, or leave the monastery and turn left onto the lane, then left into the waymarked track, Brier Lane, picking up the directions at the next three-way sign on your right.

❷ You simply cannot pass by the quaint old church, from whose entrance porch you will get a good view across to its lovely neighbour, Chithurst Manor. Leaving the church, turn left into the waysigned approach through the gates of the manor entrance. Continue on by the house and its beautiful topiary, coming out into a

small field. With a two-way sign on the right, continue down it, still with the hedge and the house garden on the left. Go over a stile into the next field and walk across to the hedge in front of you. There, go over a stile with a two-way sign and turn right. Cittaviveka and its grounds will be on your right. At the top of the field, go over the stile, bearing left into a small wood. At its end, go over another stile and, with a three-way sign facing you, turn left onto Brier Lane. It will pass by, on the right, plantations of young trees and eventually (and as if to reassure you) a three-way sign will be on the left. Just before emerging out onto Gatehouse Lane

Chithurst's Buddhist monastery

there is a two-way sign on the left.

❸ Either walk along the field path parallel to the lane or turn down Gatehouse Lane itself, to where it is about to make a junction with the A272 and there, at the give way sign, bear left into the field, then right and you are then on the field path. Please do not be tempted to cross the A272 at Corner Cottage, even though Rother Lane, our continuing route, is in sight – this is a very dangerous bend. Keep on the field path, heading towards the buildings of Trotton Farm. There the path will end at a waysign. Turn right out onto the road where it will be safe to cross as you can both see and be seen. Walk the short distance back to Rother Lane and

turn left into it. Then, with two entrance ways on the right, one is into Mill Farm, walk straight ahead onto the continuing lane.

❹ You are now approaching another area of Trotton village, the first building of which will be on your left. Then, with a three-way sign and garage in front of you, turn left, going through a gateway onto a grassy track. Coming to another group of the village buildings, the grassy track gives way to gravel. After passing the old rectory, Coppers on the left and, lastly, Tuxleith, you can cross over to visit the church. Then return to the road and turn left to go over the bridge and back to the pub.

FERNHURST

Length : 3½ miles

Getting there: Fernhurst lies either side of the A286 between Midhurst and Haslemere. To reach the old part of the village, to the east of the main road, turn into Church Road at the crossroads. This is a one way system and you then leave by Hogs Hill.

Parking: Parking is available in the large car park at the village green adjacent to the Red Lion.

Maps: OS Landranger 186, Aldershot, Guildford and surrounding area; Pathfinder, Midhurst and Petworth. Starting point GR: 901284.

This village has, perhaps, the finest cricket green and sports field of any that we know – it really is magnificent with its huge expanse of green sward, bordered on the north side by extensive woodlands. Since the Second World War there has been much development here but this end of the village has retained the small concentration of old houses and cottages that border the green, a good example of which is the pub and its two immediate neighbours, Telford and Bell House; the latter complete with its bell was the old school house, whilst the former was the headmas-

FOOD and DRINK

The Red Lion at Fernhurst is a delight in every way. The parish register records an inn-keeper here in 1592 but its history is uncertain prior to that date. This freehouse has, as its speciality, the proud boast that all the food, with the exception of ice cream and chocolate, is prepared in its kitchens and is the genuine article – truly home prepared and home cooked. It is available seven days a week both at lunchtime and in the evenings. Children can be accommodated for meals and the pub has a pleasant garden. Telephone: 01428 653304.

ter's house. The large Mansion House opposite has a Victorian letterbox in its wall. Only just beyond is the Fernhurst parish church, St Margaret's, well worth a visit.

When you are ready to commence the walk, it leads away from the village green, going past the cricket pavilion to join a path through Reeth Wood where you will encounter a geographical feature of this area, very deep ghylls (ravines) that are a sight to see when the water is in spate. Just beyond Tanyard Cottage, the path changes direction, climbing gently up into Sheetland Woods, really beautiful and full of birds. This route takes you along the western flank of Blackdown, beloved by Tennyson, as was the whole of this area. Changing direction again at Sheetlands House, the path goes by a lovely property, Copyhold. The walk returns downhill to Fernhurst through open country with a good view of Blackdown.

Copyhold House and its ancient elm

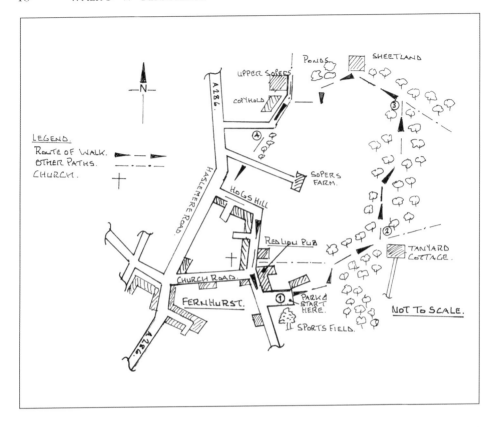

LEGEND.
ROUTE OF WALK. ▶ — ▶
OTHER PATHS. — · — · —
CHURCH. +

NOT TO SCALE.

THE WALK

❶ From the village green car park walk on past the cricket pavilion on your left to continue to the north-east corner of the field, beyond which you turn left through an opening between two oak trees. Turn right onto the track (which comes from the Red Lion pub) through Reeth Wood. Very soon you will see an example of the deep ghylls that I mentioned in the introduction. This wide track then comes to two gates, both on the left. You continue into the narrowing footpath ahead, along which you will pass by a two-way sign on the left. Then at a two-way sign on the right, and with Tanyard Cottage in front of you, turn left onto the wide woodland track of Bridge Reeds.

❷ Next at a junction of forking tracks and with a three-way sign on your right, turn into the left-hand fork. The track is now climbing gently up through the

> **PLACES of INTEREST**
>
> Tennyson's imposing house, **Aldsworth**, is on the south-east side of Blackdown. It is not open to the public, but one of the many footpaths all over this hill passes close to it. Tennyson and his family used the parish church at **Lurgashall**, south-east of Fernhurst.

woods and in a short way reaches an area partly cleared of its timber. Here, at a two-way sign on the left, bear right and continue ahead. From this cleared area you will get a good view to the right of the west flank of Blackdown. At the next two-way sign, in front of you at forking tracks, take the left-hand one. A spring-fed stream will now be on your right. At the next junction of tracks on the right, bear left. This takes you through a less wooded area. On a broad, grassy track you will pass a track junction on the right displaying the notice 'no public right of way'; you carry straight on into an avenue of young trees.

❸ At the next junction and two-way sign on the right, walk straight ahead to reach a three-way sign on your right, bringing into view a large house, Sheetlands House, and its gardens. Turn left here. This area has various outbuildings and the house and gardens are now on your right. You should have these close by you, taking you along a wide, descending track. A two-way sign is on the left and a notice asking that dogs be leashed. This track will take you down into a valley which has some lakes

and ponds. The track then ascends to a higher area, which you leave via the stile or gate, with a three-way sign opposite. Turn left onto a partly metalled lane. The house on your right is Upper Sopers. You soon come to Copyhold with its beautiful setting and views.

❹ Continue on down the lane and where it bears away to the right, and at a three-way sign on the left, walk through a gateway into a field. Keeping the hedge on your left hand, at the bottom of this field go over the stile at the gate there into the next field which has a line of oak trees down its length. You can follow these down on either side, depending on whether you want shade or not! Beyond the last tree, go over the stile at the gate at a two-way sign and the next stile on the other side of the farm track, taking you into this walk's last field, at the bottom of which is a gate. Go over this stile and in a very short way the path, which goes between houses, will bring you out onto Hogs Hill. Turn left at the waysign. There is a footway on the other side which will take you back to the pub and village green.

EASEBOURNE
Length : 3¼ miles

Getting there: Easebourne is situated about ¾ mile north of Midhurst town and the approach is via the A272 from west or east, or on the A286 from north or south. Parking: Parking is available at	the White Horse (next door to the post office) with the usual conditions. Otherwise you could park at the entrance area to Midhurst Polo Ground off the A272 and opposite the Priory, but this has to be with discretion (GR: 896225).	Maps: OS Landranger 197, Chichester and The Downs; Pathfinder, Midhurst and Petworth. Starting point GR: 897227.

Formerly, and difficult to imagine now, the village and district had very close ties with the smuggling trade and all the violence associated with it. Some dark deeds have been perpetrated here and not only by the smugglers, as in much earlier times, and affecting the local community, the excesses of the Prioress led to the Priory being dissolved, its remains now forming part of the parish church, St Mary's, which is only across the road from the pub and well worth a visit. Like Duncton, to the

---

FOOD and DRINK

There are two pubs in this village, one the Holly Tree, the other the White Horse, whose car park is an ideal starting point for this walk. Built as a coaching inn, it started life in the mid-16th century. Its patrons from those former days of trencherman meals of home-cooked food would recognise some of the choices even now, one of which is Sussex Smoked Bacon Roll. A children's menu is also available and there is quite a large adjoining garden. Meals at this friendly pub are available at lunchtime and in the evenings, seven days a week. It might be advisable to book at weekends, when the pub is well patronised by walking groups. Telephone: 01730 813521.

---

south-east, the village has a mile long street, Easebourne's being populated with picturesque stone-built houses and cottages. One feature you may find odd, if you are a stranger to Midhurst and district, is the number of dwellings whose doors, windows and fascias are painted in a very distinctive shade of yellow; the colour signifies them as belonging to the Cowdray Estate.

The walk explores the old section of the village, north of the A272, then heads west across country, when almost immediately there are wonderful views of the Downs. The route then is on enclosed woodland tracks; these and the rest of the paths are good, even in winter. There are no hills and the walk ends virtually back at the front door of the pub.

THE WALK

❶ From the pub car park turn left onto Easebourne Street. For the whole of its length you will be aware of the channelled stream to your right. On your left you will pass by the entrance to Glaziers Lane, whilst

on the right is a distinctive white, half-timbered building which is a row of three cottages, then on the left the impressive old vicarage. You continue up the lane, all the while accompanied by the sound of the tinkling stream. Then, on your left that priceless gem of institutions, the village school, and how sympathetically in keeping with its old neighbours is the main building.

❷ Coming to a junction on the left, follow the lane bearing right. Here is the first sign of the other pub, its notice board, and just around this corner is the charming Holly Tree itself. We were curious upon reaching Soutars Farm House about why it differed from the OS map place-name, with its spelling of Sowter's Farm, and what an unusual construction is Nobles Cottage on the left. On your right is a waysign and the entrance to Loves Farm where, just beyond but on the left, there is the waymarked track entrance to some cottages. Here you turn left. In only a few yards you will come to a five-bar gate. Go over the stile there and into a small field with the next stile taking you into another field. In front of you now is a fence – bear right. This takes you to its

---

PLACES of INTEREST

There is no charge for standing spectators at the **Midhurst Polo Ground** during the polo season. Only a very short way beyond the polo field are the fire gutted ruins of the original Elizabethan **Cowdray House** with a small museum close by. **Midhurst** itself is a lovely old county town with a still flourishing market. It is full of beautiful old buildings, pubs, tea rooms and restaurants. Its public library is truly a delight.

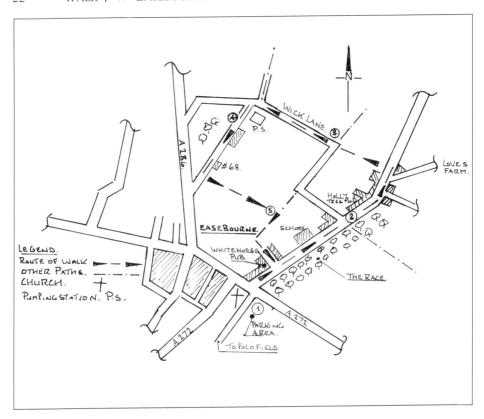

corner where, at a two-way sign, turn left to continue along by the fence on your left. At its corner, walk on up the field, mounting the distinctive ridge in it. The course of the path is obvious and you will be heading for trees a short distance away.

❸ Now as you approach the trees, you will see a gate and large oak tree. To the left of the tree in a gap in the hedge is a stile. Go over it to descend a fairly steep bank taking you down facing a lane T-junction. This is Wick Lane and a two-way sign will be on your right. Walk straight ahead – the lane is enclosed by trees but you will get occasional glimpses

of the Downs to your left. Also to your left you will have sight of a building which is a reservoir pumping station. Just beyond this, go through a gate and please ensure that you latch it behind you. Once beyond it choose the left fork. This short, descending, enclosed path will take you down to a wide track T-junction with a waysign. You turn left with main grid powerlines almost above you. In only a few steps, and with old iron estate railings on your left, turn left into a woodland track. The railings continue on the left and you will pass by the pumping station enclosure.

❹ This very pleasant descending wood-

Easebourne Street

land track continues on for some way. Then you will be reassured by the appearance on the right of a two-way sign and habitation, both on your left and straight ahead. This is all part of Easebourne. You will pass Beaufort Cottage on your left, then be reminded that you are still on the Cowdray Estate as its trademark (yellow paint) is on the next two houses on the left, the last one of which is No 68. At the end of its long garden and with its garage also on the left, turn left at the three-way sign, going up a series of steps cut in the bank at the top of which you will come out into an open field. Turn left and immediately in front of you will be a timber powerline pole; a fence and remains of a hedge will be on your left. As you approach the first pole you will see others following the same line. Continue along this field path – it is quite rough.

❺ At the end of the path there is a T-junction with a wide grassy track at a three-way sign. Turn right. As you continue you will be approaching trees and a hedge. At a gap in the hedge you will see a stile and waysign. Go by this stile to come out onto a path, facing allotment gardens. Turn left. In a short distance, and on the right, pass by a three-way sign at the corner of St Mary's graveyard. Walk on by it, then with a two-way sign on your left, the path brings you out onto a metalled lane. This is Glaziers Lane and, finally, at its junction with Easebourne Street, you turn right to the pub.

TILLINGTON, RIVER AND UPPERTON

Length : 6¾ miles

Getting there: Tillington lies about 1 mile west of Petworth on the A272.	the north of the village store and pub. Please do not park in the forecourt of the village hall.	Chichester and The Downs; Pathfinder, Midhurst and Petworth. Starting point GR: 963220.
Parking: On the road verges to	Maps: OS Landranger 197,	

This is a magnificent walk, over gorgeous rolling countryside. You will go through old Tillington, out into the open country beyond and then into the parkland of Pitshill with its variety of specimen trees. The route then takes you by imposing Pitshill House, one time home of the Mitford family and completed in 1794.

From the house the way continues through woodlands to the hamlet of River, another lovely old place, and on across River Common, then through the woods of Upperton Common and back to Tillington via neighbouring Upperton.

The parish church of All Hallows is a unique building, not only in Sussex but the whole of England, in that its tower is surmounted by a Scots crown of flying arches, an adornment found on church towers north of the border. The English painter J. M. W. Turner designed the structure for his friend and mentor, Egremont of Petworth. You simply cannot go to Tillington and not visit its church.

THE WALK

❶ From your parking place in Upperton Road walk down to the village stores to use the elevated walkway which goes by the front of the Horse Guards and from where you will get a good view of the church. This takes you to Cemetery Lane.

Then, with number 535 Old Manor House on the left, you will be facing the lychgate into the graveyard. You will note that the gate is one of a vanishing type that still has a coffin platform. Here you have a choice of following the waysigned path through the graveyard, coming out through its other gate, or continuing the short way on the lane. Then, at the gate, walk into the signposted field path opposite. Once in this large open field, you make for the farm buildings ahead of you. However, as you

proceed on the clearly defined path, you will come to a fork in it – take the right-hand one. This will bring you nearer to the hedge on your right. There you mount a bank in the field, taking you onto the higher level of the next one.

Upperton Farm is now in clear view and you continue on the well-defined path which takes you by a timber-fenced horse paddock, heading for a hedge in front of you. At the end of the fence you come out onto a lane. Cross over, going slightly to the right, and descend a flight of steps to take those opposite. Go through the wicket gate and there, with a two-way sign, walk on across this area of open ground now with good views over to the Downs on the left. Coming to a three-way sign on the left, walk straight on; a hedge will be on that side also and you will see isolated buildings head of you. Coming to a field gate at a waysign bringing you out onto New Road, walk into the lane junction on the opposite side, with the buildings of Boughton Dairy Farm on your left. Just beyond the farm track, on your left, turn right at the waysign which will take you into Dene Dip Woods.

❷ At the other end of the wood, go over a stile at a waysign and head for a timber

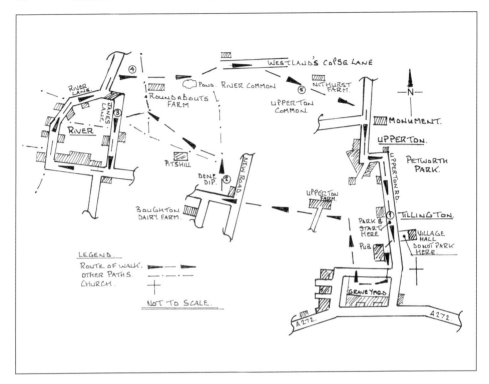

powerline pole a short way away. This will take you onto a raised level in this field, where, looking slightly left, you will see gates and a waysign. If you make for these you will see the metalled lane leading to them. To your left is the handsome mansion of Pitshill. On reaching the gates (and to avoid the cattle grid) go through the wicket gate, with a three-way sign on the right.

At a junction and three-way sign, both on the right, carry straight on into a rhododendron-lined stretch of lane. So lovely in May. Coming to the walled garden of Pitshill on the left with a garden gate, bear right at the three-way sign now on your right and almost immediately bear left (do not take the right-hand path). In

only a few paces, on your left, there is another three-way sign; walk straight ahead. Once again, in only a few paces, you will come to a fork in the path. Be sure to take the right-hand one. In summer you may find a profusion of bracken along here but it is intermittent and there are good open, wider stretches also, and the course of the path is clear on the ground. You come to yet another three-way sign, on your right and at a fork in the path. Take the left one and carry straight on.

At the next three-way sign, on the left, take the left-hand fork. Your next landmark will be a house down in the valley to your right; again you will be at a fork in the path. Be sure to take the left-hand one. This, in a very short way brings you

Pitshill House, one-time home of the Mitford family

onto another path, where you turn left. This will broaden out and lead you to another three-way sign on your right – take its left fork.

❸ You are now in Janes Lane, with an earth and stone boundary wall and trees on your right and open ground beyond. This very ancient track takes you by, on your right, a gateway and waysign on the left. Through another gateway on the right you will see a house, the first sight of River hamlet; continue on the old track, which becomes sunken. In only a short distance you pass between a two-way sign and a stile – continue ahead. Coming to a waysign, stile and gate on the right, walk on towards the houses you can see ahead of you. You

are still in Janes Lane and here it becomes metalled. These houses are part of River. Janes Lane makes a junction with another, River Lane. Turn right and you almost immediately go by another junction on your left. Walk on down River Lane with impressive, stone-built River House on your right. Beyond 'One High Bank' on the right, pass a waysign also on the right, followed by two more (one on either hand) and yet another one on the right. Perhaps there was a connection between Old Janes (on the right) and Janes Lane. Now, almost at the northern limit of the hamlet, an old farm complex is on the left, whilst on your right is the signposted entrance of Great Yew Cottage. Turn right into this partly metalled track going through woodland.

After about 400 yards, at a two-way sign on the left, turn left into the woodland path. Very shortly you will come to a rarity, a five-way sign. Here, to ensure that you make no mistake, have the waysign on your left-hand side and walk ahead into the right-hand track.

❹ In only a few paces pass a timber power-line pole on the left. Then you emerge onto an area of open ground, River Common. To your left are farm and other buildings and you then approach the buildings of Roundabouts Farm. At a two-way sign close by the farm, turn left on a wide farm track which brings you to a four-way junction of tracks, the left-hand one sign-posted to Field Cottage. Continue straight ahead. There is a four-way sign here but at the time of writing it was incorrectly positioned. You come shortly to a pond on the right. Pass the entrance to Bucks Cottage on the left, then with a three-way sign on the right, turn right. This is Westland's Copse Lane. Coming almost immediately to another three-way sign on the right, turn right onto the woodland path of Upperton Common, which climbs gently and after some way passes a two-way sign on the right. Go over a makeshift bridge across a ditch, and then another similar one. Next, you go over a rough ramp leading into a field. There, through a gate on the left, you will see the buildings of Nithurst Farm.

❺ After you cross a third makeshift bridge over a ditch, the woodland path begins to climb more steeply. In about ¼ mile and at a two-way sign you come out onto the metalled surface of Upperton Road, with Petworth Park monument in front of you. Turn right. The park boundary wall is on your left. Passing a waysign and path on the right you come to a lane junction also going off to the right. Continue on the road. As you round a bend in it the first buildings of Upperton hamlet come into view, most of which are yet more examples of fine old stone-built houses. At a red telephone kiosk on the right, at Home Farm House, bear left, still on the road. Rounding this bend, you should cross over to the pavement on the left. This will take you by, on the same side, an entrance way into Petworth Park. Then, with the last house in the hamlet, Windrush, on the right, also the sports field, recreational area and cricket pavilion, to prove that you are not far from the end of this lovely walk, you have a grand view of Tillington's church less than ¼ mile distant and continue gently downhill to your parking place in the village.

DUNCTON

Length: 2½ or 3¼ miles

Getting there: Duncton is on the A285 south of the A272 at Pet-worth. Approaching from the A27, head north on the A285 at Maudlin, east of Chichester.

Parking: The walk starts by the Cricketers Arms, where there is ample parking, with the usual proviso. An alternative is Willett Close in the centre of the village (GR: 960173).

Maps: OS Landranger 197 Chichester and The Downs; Pathfinder, Cocking and Sutton. Starting point GR: 960170.

English villages, and certainly those in Sussex, come in all configurations of shape and size – round, square, short and long. The latter description is certainly true of Duncton, but despite the length of its High Street, it is noticeably short of dwellings. Be assured, however, that its beauty is behind the scenes and away from the road

to the east. As with so many other villages close to the coast and in particular to Chichester, this area was used by the Romans and in 1815 a Roman military hypocaust was found here that had heated the water to refresh weary soldiers. No doubt the spring you will see at Duncton Mill supplied the water. The site of the

FOOD and DRINK

The 16th-century Cricketers Arms is at the south end of the village and is everyone's concept of a village pub – full of old world charm and comfort, with an enormous horse chestnut tree as its immediate neighbour. It has an adjoining skittle alley and beautiful gardens at both back and front, the latter with a play area. I have no doubt that if you visit in the summertime you will be drawn back in the winter when this cosy pub is even cosier with its enormous open inglenook fire blazing. There are full à la carte and bar food menus, all made from fresh produce and to order, and barbecues at Sunday lunchtimes during the summer. Telephone: 01903 871337.

Roman baths is close to Manor Farm, on the route of the extended part of this walk; sadly no trace of the bath house building remains but if, like me, you stop and listen very carefully you may hear the voices of the people and the sound of them disporting themselves in the water!

The walk goes up by the parish church, Holy Trinity, where there is a handsome memorial to a lady prominent in the Women's Suffragette Movement. You will continue to the Roman Catholic church and across the fields to Burton church and St Michaels Burton Park. Beyond the southern end of Burton Ponds you reach Duncton's marvellous old mill and pond and the biggest trout you're ever likely to see. At this point the walk can be extended by ¼ mile. The going is all over good, firm paths and tracks, there is one gentle climb . . . the views are SPECTACULAR!

THE WALK

❶ Assuming you have taken advantage of the parking offered at the pub, you should walk north from it and cross over the road opposite the police house, continuing on the pavement on the west side. Then, with the village hall on the left, shortly beyond and on the right are the massive wrought iron entrance gates to St Michaels Burton Park, formerly a girls' school, more recently a police dog training centre and now private dwellings.

You will find Willett Close on your left. If you have parked here this can be your starting point. Just beyond you will see the steeple of the parish church. Proceed ahead and, in only a few yards, turn left to go through a wicket gate set in the hedge; now in a meadow, walk across to the wicket gate opposite to enter the churchyard. This church, typically Victorian, was built in 1866. It replaced the very much older St Mary's from which one bell was salvaged and installed in the 'new' church. This bell, cast in 1364, is thought to be the oldest one in England. There is a memorial as you approach the entrance porch of more modern significance, to Florence Gertrude de Fonblanque (1864–1949), the originator and leader of the Women's Suffragette march from

PLACES of INTEREST

Just north of Duncton is the grand old town of **Petworth**, full of alleyways, passages and twittens not open to motor traffic. There are many pubs, cafés, tea rooms and more antique shops than in any place of comparable size that I know. But of course the jewel in the crown is **Petworth House** (NT) and its park.

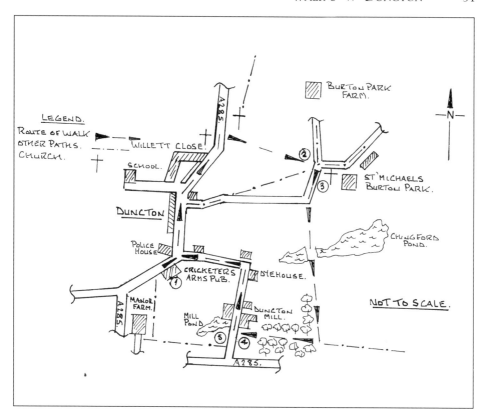

Edinburgh to London in 1912.

From the churchyard, walk out onto the lane and turn right. Then, with the Old School House on the right, cross over the road to the pavement on its east side. With a cluster of cottages on the left across the road, bear right into a fenced path which will take you down by the Catholic church on your left. Walk on beyond the church and there, with a three-way sign on your left, go through a Victorian kissing-gate and continue on a field path.

❷ Coming into view ahead will be the buildings of St Michaels Burton Park and Burton church. Even more impressive, of course, are the views to your right of the wooded slopes of Duncton Hill. You will be walking towards very old Spanish sweet chestnut trees and there go over a stile to continue ahead on the field path. The open parkland spreads out on either side of the path and to your left you will see Burton Park Farm. At a four-way sign in front, go over the stile and turn right onto the metalled surfaced lane. You are now only a few yards away from one of the loveliest old churches in Sussex (also one of the smallest and full of treasures); built in 1075 and not dedicated. Its next door neighbour, the mansion of Burton Park, was built by the Courtauld Family.

A memorial to a brave lady

❸ Leaving the church, walk back out to the metalled lane and turn left onto it, with a three-way sign on your right. You will then pass by the driveway, on your left, to St Michaels with its columned frontage. Shortly beyond, and with another three-way sign on the right, still continue ahead. To your front, of course, will be the thickly wooded north face of Duncton Hill. Where the metalled lane makes a sharp bend to the right, walk straight ahead through a gateway with a two-way sign on the left and continue down this field path towards the trees in front. As you reach them you will find they were concealing the western extremity of Burton Ponds. At this point you have to go through a cast iron gate; a bridge takes you across the spillway. Emerging into an open field with a two-way sign on the left, walk towards the trees in front of you – Fountain Copse. On reaching the wood, the ascending path has the trees on your right and open countryside on the left. At the top of this path, with a three-way sign facing you, turn hard right and walk into a path which is enclosed by hedges on either hand, and start to descend with an old orchard on your right and a glimpse of Duncton Mill beyond. The path will descend quite steeply to Duncton Mill Lane and, with a three-way sign on the left, you now have a choice of route back to your starting point – either one will bring you out just by (above or below) the pub at Duncton.

❹ Whichever is your choice, you MUST turn right and walk the short distance to the mill and its pond. Hopefully you will have brought your camera with you to capture this magnificent place. You will, no doubt, be incredulous at the huge rainbow trout (which are not fished for) cruising about in the 'gin-clear' water of the pond. On your right is the old mill and, looking over its wall, one can see the mill wheel still in position but sadly no longer functioning. If it is your intention to continue on this slightly shorter route back to the pub, then simply walk on along the lane and go through a gate, taking you on past the man-made trout fishing ponds on the left. Your next landmark is Dyehouse, set in its beautiful wild garden and, as you will hear, watered by its own fast running stream. Beyond this point no further directions are necessary as the lane quite simply carries on to the A285, where it comes out along a short way north of the Cricketers pub.

❺ If, however, you decide to take the slightly longer route, walk back up to the waysign where you came out onto the lane and continue beyond it, with a hedge on your right and at about halfway along its length a waysign. Turn right over the stile into a large field to walk across it on the clearly defined path. When you top the rise, there in front of you are the buildings of Manor Farm which, when you reach them, will have a three-way sign. You turn right here and head north. The farm buildings will be on your left, and as you leave the last of them, you may like to know that the Roman military bath house would have been in the field now on your right (although this site is not identified in any way). The path continues over stiles, its direction confirmed by waysigns. You will go across a stream on a footbridge and shortly beyond come out almost into the pub car park.

SLINDON

Length : 1½ or 6 miles

Getting there: Coming south on the A29, pass the Spur pub on the left and at the Slindon crossroads turn west (Reynolds Lane). Approaching from the A27, go north at Fontwell racecourse round-about, joining the A29. In about ½ mile turn west where sign-posted to Slindon at the cross-roads.

Parking: You can park at the layby opposite the entrance gates to Slindon House School. If this is full, use the area oppo-site the Roman Catholic church a few yards to the east.

Maps: OS Landranger 197, Chichester and The Downs; Pathfinders, Chichester and Bognor, and Cocking and Sutton. Starting point GR: 960086.

This lovely village is largely owned by the National Trust. The layout of the old part, to the west of the A29, is roughly a dissected circle and just made for walking around, and should this be your first visit, I'll guarantee that it will not be your last. If you come in the autumn, don't miss the magnificent display of pumpkins cultivated at No 4 Top Road (Pumpkin Cottage). There were settlements here in prehistoric

FOOD and DRINK

The village itself has one pub, the Newburgh Arms dating from around 1700. A wide selection of bar meals is available. Telephone: 01243 814229. There is a garden, and a Parish Council children's play area lies just beyond the pub but supervision of children there is, of course, advisable.

times and a local ploughman has amassed a collection of over 900 Stone Age tools he has turned up in the fields, some of which are on loan to Chichester Museum. A visit to St Mary's church is an absolute must. Amongst other interesting relics, it contains the only carved timber effigy in a Sussex church, that of Sir Anthony St Leger, which has survived the centuries well. There is also a commemorative plaque to Stephan Langton, Archbishop of Canterbury, who died in Slindon in 1228. More recently, various houses in the village have been home to Hilaire Belloc, the Sussex poet and author, and his family.

The walk takes you on a circuit of old Slindon (about 1½ miles) before striking out on tracks and wooded paths into the beautiful countryside to the north of the village, passing Nore Folly with splendid views over the English Channel.

THE WALK

❶ From your parking place opposite Slindon House School, or at the RC church, we first take you around the village. Walk east and, coming to the junction of Top Road and Church Hill, perhaps you will take in the atmosphere of the village on the seat around the (young) chestnut tree at this location. Turn right down Church Hill. There on the left is The

Old Inn House, the original pub, whilst opposite is No 11 The Old Post House and, just beyond, the parish church, St Mary's, dating from 1087. Opposite the entrance porch is a rare cork bark oak tree; we know of only two others in West Sussex, at West Stoke church and in the grounds of Stedham House.

Pass the church and on the left lies a Victorian summer house, an old railway carriage with a thatched roof! With Dyers Lane on your left, The Grange (the last home in Slindon of Madame Belloc) is on your right. Just beyond this impressive house is the charming village pond. Continue into Church Road and, with the village stores on the right, you will come to the junction of Reynolds Lane and School Hill (the location of the old village pump). Bear left into School Hill. Gaston Farm is on the right. The Newburgh Arms is on the same side of the road and opposite the pub is the old school.

❷ Bear left into Top Road – what a picture postcard subject Slindon post office makes on the right with its thatch, with the Old Bakery just beyond. Coming to

PLACES of INTEREST

Both Chichester (the capital of West Sussex) and Arundel can be reached via the A27 in a few minutes from Slindon. **Chichester** still has the extensive remains of the original Roman walls and the Bishops Palace Gardens, adjacent to the cathedral, are particularly attractive. There are signposted walks round both the walls and the gardens. Lovely **Arundel**, with its continental atmosphere, has its castle, park and nearby Wildfowl and Wetlands Trust reserve.

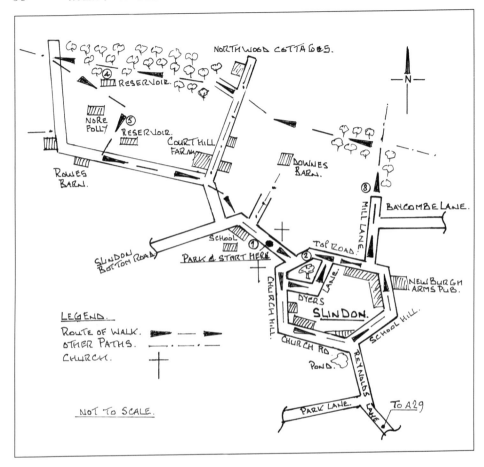

the junction with Mill Lane, on the right, continue on Top Road. Next on the left is Bleak House, the first home in Slindon of the Belloc family as its commemorative plaque confirms. Go on by the junction of Dyers Lane on the left to continue on Top Road and there on the left is No 4 (Pumpkin Cottage). Now back at the junction with Church Hill, walk on into it and continue down to Dyers Lane. Turn left. Through the open gates of Mulberry House you will catch a glimpse of its magnificent gardens. At the junction of the

lane with Top Road you can either return to your car or continue into the countryside. If the latter is your choice, then turn right onto Top Road and, with Bleak House now on your right, walk the short distance to Mill Lane and turn left onto it.

❸ In only about 300 yards (where the lane bears sharply right) walk past a field gate at a waysign into the wide track beyond. As you reach its high point the views begin to open up. There, to your left, is Nore Hill and you will catch your

Granny annex, Slindon style

first sight of the folly. With the track then descending you come to a three-way sign. Walk ahead to a gate and waysigns in front of you – one waysign reads 'bridle road to Bignor'. To your right are views across Dale Park. Here bear left on the grassy track with a fence on your right. A three-way sign is on your left and you carry on to the next three-way sign now in front of you. There walk straight on and, passing a two-way sign, continue in the same direction. At the next two-way sign, turn left. The track descends into lovely open countryside. Then, coming to an old gateway with a waysign just beyond, walk straight ahead. The track emerges onto a metalled lane; turn right. Next, where the lane forks and with two-way and a National

Trust sign in front, take the left-hand fork onto a stony track. Here, through the trees to your right, you will see the buildings of Northwood Farm and cottages. The woodland track brings you to a three-way sign on the left. Walk through a wicket gate. The now gently rising track brings you to a three-way sign on the left – here turn left.

❹ With the track still climbing gently, at the next three-way sign on the right, turn left. At the top of the rise and at yet another three-way sign, bear left onto the public footpath; the fingerboard excludes cyclists. Continue on this wider track, the surface of which has been paved with chalk and can be slippery when wet. Once more at a three-way sign on the left, bear left, going by a pole gate, watching your footing. The wide track continues through Nore Wood and you will pass a two-way sign on the right. Coming eventually to another pole gate at a two-way sign, go through the steel gate beyond and follow the stone track taking you down to Nore Folly on the right. This structure was built by Samuel Refoy in 1814 for Countess Newburgh; only quite recently did the family building firm of Refoys in Bognor cease to exist. From this point there are views across the coastal plain and over the English Channel.

❺ Continue now down the wide, stony track built by the Portsmouth Water Company to give access to its various reservoirs hereabouts. Look across to Halnaker Hill to your right to get a lovely view of its mill, both much loved and written about by Hilaire Belloc. At a track junction turn left (it is sometimes muddy along here). Walk down to Courthill Farm where you go through a gateway and out onto a metalled lane. Turn right. You need now to be vigilant for in just about 100 yards you turn sharp left through a gap in the hedge. Take this un-waymarked permissive path which runs parallel to and above the lane and in a few minutes brings you to your car.

SUTTON

Length: 4 miles

Getting there: Coming from the south, take the A29 and at the Bury crossroads turn off west, signposted to Bignor Roman Villa, with Sutton beyond. From the north, take the A285 out of Petworth. Just beyond Heath End turn east, signposted to Burton Mill, Sutton and Bignor

Roman Villa. From wherever the approach is made to Sutton, take care on the very narrow country roads.

Parking: You may park (carefully) in the street just north of the pub and village hall. If you are visiting the White Horse you

can use the pub car park or its overspill at the village hall while you walk, but please ask first.

Maps: OS Landranger 197, Chichester and The Downs; Pathfinder, Cocking and Sutton. Starting point GR: 979151.

The old village of Sutton lies mainly between its church and pub, with possibly ¼ mile between the two. There are many lovely houses to be seen, among them the former school. At the end of the walk you go through the garden (on the legal right of way, of course) of magnificent Beckhall, which I consider to be one of the very finest examples of 16th-century architecture in West Sussex. The parish church, St

FOOD and DRINK

Sutton's one pub, the White Horse, which is very popular with walkers, has deeds going back to 1746 but is probably older, and has always had its present day name – unusual for pubs. It is a free-house with a restaurant for which it has a good reputation in the area. Fish is a speciality, this being obtained fresh every day, weather permitting, from markets on the coast. There is a good vegetarian choice and children's menus are available. Food is served seven days a week both at lunchtime and in the evenings. Telephone: 01798 869221.

John's, is itself a beautiful old building, well restored during the 19th century. The walk continues beyond it, with splendid views of the north face of the Downs, along whose skyline ridge runs the South Downs Way. Your next landmark will be Barlavington, a tiny hamlet consisting of a church, large farm and more handsome houses! I have a 'thing' about trees – all trees, but especially yews. The county has many huge, venerable examples of the species, and just beyond Barlavington church you will pass one of the biggest, many centuries old. You return to Sutton via Folly Lane (what Folly, I wonder?) and field paths.

THE WALK

❶ You start by walking north up the village street, passing Forge House. Coming almost to the church, on the right is School House, sympathetically converted. To get a better view of the old school, just go a little way into School Lane. With Heriots on the left, turn into the churchyard next door. Note, just after you enter, the flight of stone steps on your left which

you must come back to if you visit the church itself, a surprisingly large building to serve such a small community.

❷ Return to the steps and turn right, walking towards a gate in the opposite wall beyond which you turn right onto the wide track and are immediately aware of the towering Downs, quite spectacular. Walk on; then, with a waysign on the right, turn right onto a footpath. Normally, you would go over a stile here but, unless it has been repaired by the time you do this walk, you can bypass it through a gap in the fence. Proceed down the field – a wood will be on your right as will a gateway and waysign. The path descends into a small wood. At the next stile, which has also been bypassed, the path goes down to a footbridge over a stream and stile. Cross this into a meadow. Bear right at the two-way sign heading up to the next stile now in sight in the hedge and go through this contraption. Turn left and, with a hedge partway on your left, walk up the field path, then as you top the rise the buildings of Barlavington Farm appear. You come out at the farm, facing its barns.

PLACES of INTEREST

Like Bosham, Sutton also has very close Roman associations and what splendid remains they left for us to marvel at Bignor, to the south. The large **Roman Villa** was discovered in 1811 and subsequently excavated and protected under beautifully thatched houses, the mosaic floors giving those at Fishbourne a close run for their money. The villa is open to the public from June to September every day from 10 am to 6 pm and there is a very pleasant cafeteria.

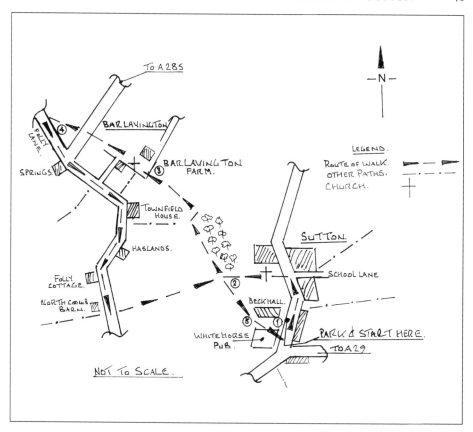

❸ There, with a two-way sign on the right, turn left onto the farm lane. You will catch a glimpse of the parish church of St Mary on your right. Then pass by on the same side a three-way sign and almost immediately a two-way sign on the left and here you turn left going through a wicket gate into the churchyard. You leave by the other wicket gate to turn left once again onto the farm lane and right onto the gravel driveway to a large stables. There will be a two-way sign and wicket gate facing you. Go through it and proceed on the footpath. The descending path leads to a two-way sign at a footbridge; go

over it, cross the lane, climb up a series of steps opposite and go over the stile. The path continues into a field with a hedge on the right. Where the hedge ends the path continues across the field and facing you will be a copper beech tree beneath which you will see waysigns and a stile. Turn left into Folly Lane.

❹ With a lane junction going off to the left, continue on Folly Lane. Passing by a waysign on the left and another at the entrance way into Townfield House, your next landmark will be Haslands Farm and Farm House. Rounding another bend in

Magnificent Beckhall

the lane, you suddenly encounter Folly Cottage. Then for several hundred yards it is as though one is walking through a tunnel with the tree branches meeting overhead. Shortly beyond this you come to a crossing track, leading on the right into Northcomb Barn; a two-way sign is concealed in the hedge here. You now turn left, going for a few yards up a steep, rough track which levels out onto a wide field track. This brings you to a four-way sign on the left which you should recognise, and here you turn right onto a field path. Now you will be heading towards trees, above which (as you draw nearer) you will see the roof and chimneys of a large house. Then, coming to the trees, hedge and a two-way sign (if you have a dog with you

please ensure it is leashed), go through the kissing-gate to emerge into a garden. The roof and chimneys, as you now see, belong to 16th-century Beckhall. With the gate directly behind you, continue straight down the garden. You will pass by a cupressus hedge on your left, then a stone building, beyond which is a narrow footpath.

❺ Go down a set of concrete steps, into the backyard of Beckhall, and continue through the gate set in the wall to your right (please fasten this and the next gate, behind you). Now, in a narrow, enclosed path and passing by a large house and beautiful wild garden, you will shortly go through the second wicket gate and reach the backyard of the White Horse.

27/5/13

Lovely walk although
really need trainers
for across the fields.
DON'T try to return via
castle (private prop) or
eat at Riverside Cafe –
slow, expensive + any
cake.
(Just use toilets
there)

WALK 9

AMBERLEY

Length: 2¼ or 6 miles

Getting There: From the A29 turn east into the B2139, signposted to Houghton and Storrington. Amberley lies approximately 1½ miles east of Houghton. Alternatively, from the A24 turn west at the Washington roundabout into the A283, signposted to Storrington and Pulborough. At Storrington, take the B2139, signposted to Amberley, Houghton and Arundel. Amberley lies approximately 4 miles west of Storrington.

Parking: A car parking area is available at the church, or you could park along Church Street itself. There is a voluntary contribution box on the wall of the parochial hall wall! The village pub has only 'on-street' parking.

Maps: OS Landranger 197, Chichester and The Downs; Pathfinder, Pulborough and Steyning. Starting point GR: 028132.

Despite this village having to suffer the plague of the motor car, it is absolutely beautiful. I describe West Chiltington as having 'as fine a collection of old stone- built and half-timbered dwellings as you're likely to see in Sussex, West or East' – here you will find the best collection of thatched cottages and houses of any vil-

FOOD and DRINK

Amberley's pub, the 17th-century Black Horse, is a colourful, charming old place, complete in one bar with its original flagstone floor. It has a pleasant garden and a large restaurant and offers a very wide range of food produced from fresh ingredients and cooked to order – the lobster meals are a sight for sore eyes. There is also a children's menu. Food is available every day of the week, both at lunchtime and in the evening. Telephone: 01798 831700.

There is another pub to the east of Amberley at Cross Gates and also one at Houghton Bridge, as well as the tea rooms, and last but not least, the acclaimed restaurant at Amberley Castle.

lage in the whole of Sussex, probably in the South of England! Most of the properties have wonderful, colourful gardens during spring and summer – it has to be an artists'/photographers' paradise. The main area of the village is concentrated along Church Street, Hog Alley, High Street and Hog Lane with the route of this easy, level walk starting from the church and returning there, having taken in most of the village. The parish church of St Michael is very ancient and still retains some Norman windows. As you continue away from the church down to the village pond, you pass the massive northern aspect wall of Amberley Castle. For most of its existence this place has been in the ownership of ecclesiastics, but is now in private hands and tours of the building can be arranged by appointment at no charge. The number to call is 01798 831992.

You then go out across the water meadows with fine views of Bury village – right up to the very last moment before going up to the river bank it looks as if you could

walk there but, of course, the river intervenes. Why then does the third finger of the waysign point that way? A ferry boat was once available but sadly was discontinued. At this point you have the choice of simply retracing your way back to Amberley, with all the quite different views this new approach will give you, or of continuing on the river bank, as directed by the waysigns, to Houghton Bridge. The route is quite straightforward and will bring you out at the Houghton Bridge Tea Rooms, from where you return to Amberley on the same path. This adds 3¼ miles to the walk, all on level ground. It is, perhaps, best done in summer as the going underfoot can be wet in winter.

THE WALK

❶ Leaving the church car park, head east down Church Street and immediately to the right and left are two magnificent houses, one of which is thatched. Next on the right is one of the old village farmsteads now beautifully restored and converted to private dwellings. Is it in appreciation that the cottage opposite is called Barn View? As you pass the junction of Hog Alley on the left, on the right is the pottery, formerly a chapel house. Next on the left you pass by one way into Hog Lane. Continuing down Church

PLACES of INTEREST

There can be few museums housed in such a location as **Amberley Chalk Pits Museum** and it is amazing just how many trades from times past are represented here. The museum is open all year round and has its own cafeteria. The entrance fee includes car parking.

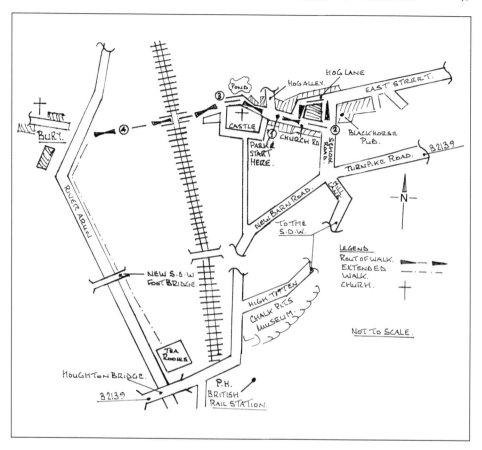

Street, on the opposite side is a public footpath leading to the recreation field. Coming to the old bakery you will note that part of the original guttering system has survived and is mounted on the front wall, 1794 being the casting date.

❷ At the junction of Church Street, School Road and High Street, turn left into the latter, shortly to pass (on the right) the entrance to the village store, housed in a restored and converted barn, part of the farm complex that was on this site. At the Black Horse turn left into Hog Lane (the road going right, East Street, has some old houses for a short distance along it, but soon comes to the more modern, postwar area of Amberley). North Road Farm is on the left and opposite is Brook Green. You then pass, on the right, a waysign pointing in the direction of 'The Wey South Path', which goes north from here across Amberley Wild Brooks, an area which it is not advisable to walk over in winter. This 35 mile long path runs from Bramber to Guildford. With Old Place on the right, turn right into Church Street and return to the church.

Hog Lane, Amberley

❸ Continue now on the metalled lane, the last bit of Church Street. The village pond is at the bottom and shortly beyond it you pass the north wall of Amberley Castle. One feature you cannot fail to notice is what appears to be a huge buttress (which it is) but also served as a refuse and nightsoil chute! You will also note that the two apertures at the bottom would be unbreachable during time of siege. Where the metalled lane bends sharply left, walk on into the footpath going straight ahead, giving good views over to Bury village, and to your right will be Timberley Farm and cottages. The path then comes to the railway crossing and continues beyond on a wide grassy track.

❹ Coming to a steel gate with a two-way sign, go over the stile there and, bearing slightly left, walk across this field to the next waysign. Go across the earth bridge into the next field, making for the next waysign. Go over the stile and bridge, heading for the three-way sign mounted on the Arun river bank path. As you get up onto it you will see the concrete staging used for the ferry to keep passengers dry footed in times of high water or flood conditions. At the waysign, you have the choice of returning to Amberley from this point or continuing via the river bank path to and from Houghton Bridge. In either event you will enjoy the views, particularly of Amberley Castle as you approach from this different direction.

PATCHING

Length: 4 miles

Getting there: From the A280 south-west of Findon turn westwards, signposted to Patching (Coldharbour Lane). The beauty of the village can be more fully appreciated by approaching from the A27 to the south. At the roundabout complex turn off onto the old A27, then turn north into France Lane, just west of the Horse and Groom.

Parking: There is a parking area at the top of The Street, which continues northwards from France Lane. Alternatively, you could leave your car at the Fox – please ask first – and start the walk there (GR: 078057).

Maps: OS Landranger 197, Chichester and The Downs; Pathfinder, Worthing. Starting point GR: 089068.

A settlement was recorded here with the foundation of the church in AD 948. An ancient place indeed. This isolated and unspoilt village is enchanting, with many old thatched cottages, and the church of St John the Divine is a must to visit. Various landmarks carry the name Selden, to honour John Selden, 1584–1654, who lived at nearby Salvington. This eminent man of letters was a professional jurist, legal author, oriental scholar and historian of the English Civil War. The walk beyond the village is a total delight, over gently undulating countryside, with magnificent views from Patching Hill then on into lovely woodland tracks, the woods carpeted with bluebells in springtime.

THE WALK

❶ From the parking area go through the gate onto the track going north up Patching Hill; as you will discover, 'up' is very gentle. Then, in only a few yards, the magnificent views across the Long Furlong (Findon) Valley, with Myrtle Grove Farm to the north-east, begin to unfold and will remain for some time. As you glance back to the south-west, the village church will also keep you company. You will pass a waysign on the left and shortly beyond a 'rest awhile and take in the view' seat, a lovely place at any time of day. Continue ahead on the clearly defined path.

A busy day in France Lane

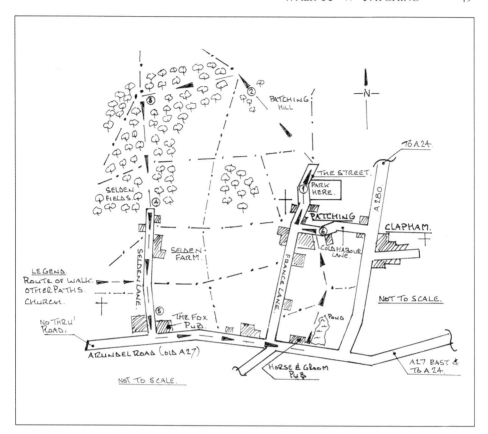

❷ The downland track goes through a group of trees and, shortly beyond, there is a fence and gate. Go to the left and you can cross the stile there and continue ahead on the wide woodland track. Then, coming to a four-way sign, go straight ahead. At the next four-way sign turn left. This delightful woodland track goes through the north end of Patching Rough and Barnstake Copse. Passing a three-way sign, go ahead to another four-way sign and turn left. Make sure you look through the trees and across the expanse of open ground to the buildings of Angmering Park Stud Farm – a splendid view.

❸ A short way past the last four-way sign and coming to a three-way sign continue ahead (do not bear into the track going right). The character of the track surface

---

PLACES of INTEREST

Findon, to the north-east, is another charming old village. Its sheep fair is held annually on Nepcote Green on the second Saturday of September. Signposted from Nepcote Green is one of the many tracks going up to **Cissbury Ring**, a huge Stone Age fort, its ramparts and ditch defences still well preserved and part of a chain along the South Downs.

changes and at all seasons it is on a good stone foundation as you go through the lovely woods of Stonyland Copse. As before ignore all the unmarked tracks to left and right and carry straight on at the next four-way sign.

❹ Eventually this track will bring you to the first buildings of Selden Farm on the left, then the farm cottages and concrete silos. With a two-way sign on the right you now continue on the metalled surface of Selden Lane, a right of way, then with the restored buildings of Old Selden Farm on the left the lane brings you to the buildings of Merrivale Fruit Farm and almost immediately out onto the old A27 road.

❺ Here, on your left, is the Fox, nicely placed at a little over halfway through the walk. We continue left beyond this pub on the old road, using the walkway on the south side of it. Then, coming to the Horse and Groom, cross over the road and walk onto the waymarked path just beyond the pub buildings. This enclosed path comes to a two-way sign. Go over the stile here, bringing you out into a long open meadow (this is a horse pasture and

dogs have to be leashed). A hedge is on your left and Patching Pond on the right. Still with the hedge on the left, go by a three-way sign and stile set in the hedge; you will have seen Patching church spire come into view. Before reaching the end of the meadow, turn right, cross it and head for the stile and waysign set in the hedge. Having gone over the stile, walk up to the four-way sign in front of you and there turn left, making now for the stile and waysign in front of you. Over the stile, you will find yourself back in the original meadow; now make for the metal gate in the opposite corner and go over the stile there at the waysign.

❻ On this last field path, walk over to the houses on the opposite side. The path goes through the houses and comes out onto Coldharbour Lane – there turn left. At the junction of the lanes, turn right into The Street and there in a few yards you can go left towards Patching Farm and the church.

On returning from the church, turn left into The Street for a quiet wander back to the parking area.

WEST CHILTINGTON

Length: 2 miles

Getting there: From the A29 turn east at Pulborough onto the A283. At Marehill turn off towards Nutbourne, just south of which turn right, signposted to West Chiltington. If approaching on the B2139, turn west at Picketty Cottages, signposted to the village. Take care as all approaches are on narrow country lanes.

Parking: You can park at the Elephant and Castle, the walk's starting point, but please ask first. Alternatively, there is limited parking near the entrance to the church.

Maps: OS Landranger 197, Chichester and The Downs, and 198, Brighton and The Downs; Pathfinder, Pulborough and Steyning. Starting point GR: 090182.

This village has everything – two pubs, the most beautiful medieval church, stocks, whipping post, museum, windmill and as fine a collection of old stone-built and half-timbered dwellings as you're likely to see in Sussex, West or East. Oh! and that rarity these days . . . a thriving village shop and post office, very conveniently sited near one of the pubs.

From the Elephant and Castle we

FOOD and DRINK

The Elephant and Castle is a very pleasant, comfortable and welcoming pub with a fascinating history. Ceiling meat hooks from when it was a butcher's premises can still be seen. There is a large, safe garden with enclosed children's play area and aviaries; the landlord breeds and releases barn owls into the wild. A large choice of food is offered, all prepared from fresh ingredients and cooked to order. Telephone: 01798 813307. The walk also goes near the Rising Sun at Nutbourne and the Queens Head, back in the village.

direct you up Church Street and into the churchyard. The stocks and whipping post, circa 1650, are close by its gate and well preserved. The church really is a gem, built between 1100 and 1150 on the site of the previous Saxon one, and its extensive wall murals have been well preserved, not ruined by Victorian conservators as was the case in so many other churches.

The walk continues into open countryside and on past soft fruit fields and Chiltington's huge windmill, now a private residence. Built elsewhere, dismantled and rebuilt on this site, this smock mill last worked in the 1920s.

Further on, Fryars Vineyard, with its garden of topiary specimens, has to be seen to be believed. It is so beautiful. We continue past more of the village's old houses before heading towards the old watermill at Nutbourne and the tower of its windmill. This lovely walk returns to West Chiltington across the golf course and, coming out at Kings and Princes Farm, gives you a chance to enjoy the rest of the village north of the church and perhaps visit the museum.

THE WALK

❶ From the pub walk up into Church Street; the museum is on your left and, with Church House on the right, bear left by the stocks, whipping post and village sign. Here turn into the churchyard. Of the church itself it has been said, 'if West Chiltington church was in Italy, people would make pilgrimages to it' . . . how true. Coming out from the building, turn left onto a paved path, go through the kissing-gate and, with a three-way sign on the left and churchyard wall on the right, walk straight on. Then at a junction of paths with a four-way sign on the left, turn left – with an old wall on your right. Go through a gateway with a number of modern houses on the left and continue into open fields. Then with a three-way sign and two stiles on the left, the path takes you on to go over a stile. The fruit and berry orchards of Church Field Farm will now be on your left, still with open ground on the right. Coming to a stile at a pole gate (simply slide the pole back and replace it), walk on down the field path, along which and looking to your right you will catch your

PLACES of INTEREST

Just to the south-west of West Chiltington, on the A283, is the RSPB property and reserve at **Uppertons Barn** which has been beautifully restored and contains numerous facilities for RSPB members including a cafeteria and shops which are open to the public. For members this is the wildfowl centre on the Pulborough and Amberley Wild Brooks (water meadows). The Sussex Trust for Nature Conservation also owns large sections of the water meadows and the whole area is quite well served by public footpaths.

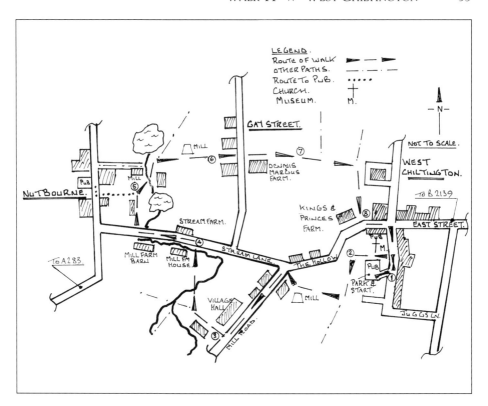

first view of West Chiltington's windmill. With a stile, gate and waysign on the left, go through the gate here, then with a very large oak tree on the right and three-way sign on the left, turn right. Now on a stone and dirt track through another area of the fruit farm and where the continuing trackway bends sharply left, walk straight ahead onto a grassy track.

❷ Coming to a steel gate (which you can walk around) reach a two-way sign and a wall on the left. Continue down this enclosed path and quite soon you will be confronted by the huge windmill, sadly now with only two sweeps remaining; what a romantic place to live in! Just beyond the

mill at the junction with the lane, Mill House and its Victorian postbox are on the left, Malthouse and Fryars Vineyard House opposite; turn left into Mill Road. Keeping a sharp lookout for oncoming traffic from left and right, cross over as soon as possible in order to face any oncoming traffic. The old buildings now on your right were the former Lakers Farm complex and are now private houses; you will note that Lakers Farm has a date plaque – AD 1493 – old West Chiltington indeed!

❸ Pass the village hall on your right and at the waysign turn right into the car park. As you do so you will be approaching a gate leading to the large playing field. Bypass

Fryars Vineyard

the gate, keeping the pavilion building to your left, with the ditch and trees on the same side. At the corner of the field, go over the footbridge and step over a large black pipe. With a waysign in front of you, turn right over the stile. A much-used farm track goes across this field to its opposite side, crossing an earth bridge, and will bring you to a gate and waysign. Go out onto Stream Lane and turn left.

❹ The lane's namesake will keep you company on the left. We have never known this to run dry, in fact more often than not it floods the road in periods of heavy rain. Then on the right you will pass by the lovely old buildings of Stream Farm. Shortly beyond and with the entrances of

Mill Farm House and Mill Farm Barn on the left, turn right at the waysign to go up the bank here and over a stile. This will bring you into an extensive soft fruit area (no scrumping please!). The broad path with a hedge on the left takes you by a large modern house and glasshouses to a two-way sign on the right, still among the soft fruit. Continue ahead on the broad grassy track. Now on your right are trees and, beyond, a stream and large pond. You also pass by a timber garden shed on the right, just beyond the trees. At about this time you will also glimpse, through the trees, the buildings of Nutbourne watermill.

❺ Then with a three-way sign and stile on your right you have the opportunity, if you wish, to divert to the Rising Sun at Nutbourne for coffee. Some of the hamlet's buildings can be seen to your left – simply turn left and follow the waysigns the very short way out to the village street, with the pub up to your right. Return to the stile to continue the walk. Go over the stile and down the bank. Now directly facing you will be the mill ponds and there on the bank are the sad remains of some parts of the mill's machinery. Turn left into the enclosed path, going over a stile. You will get a good view of the miller's house and the other buildings. The path brings you out onto a track beyond them. Here I suggest you turn left to get a better view of the old mill, now called The Wheel House. To continue, turn back to your point of exit from the buildings and with these now on your right and a three-way sign on the left you go up the rising track, passing vineyards on either hand. To your left you will see the tower of the old windmill which operated here and like so many of its kind is now a dwelling.

❻ The track brings you to a gate and two-way sign. Go over the stile here, taking you into a cultivated field, with a line of pollarded poplar trees on your left. The path continues along by these into two more fields with two other stiles, taking you into a third and narrow field. The buildings now in front of you are part of Gay Street hamlet. Go over the stile to enter the garden and driveway of Stile Farm Cottage. When you reach the metalled lane cross straight over; a waysign will be on your left in the hedge. Go up the steps set in the bank and over the stile at the top, bringing you out into a field, with the buildings of Dennis Marcus Farm on your right. Continue down the field with the boundary hedge close by, also on the right. West Chiltington golf course is now in front of you.

❼ At the bottom corner of this field at a two-way sign and gate, go over the stile taking you onto the golf course. A length of hedge is on your left. Follow this and the broad track continues on beyond it. At a three-way sign on your right, walk straight ahead, still on the broad track. (Note: you should give way, as a matter of courtesy, to any golfers in the process of driving across this track.) Once past the last waysign, you approach a wicket gate set in a hedge. There is a three-way sign here also; go through the gate into the sunken and tree-lined path.

❽ Shortly, and with another three-way sign facing you, turn right. This path will bring you out at Kings and Princes Farm on your right. Shortly beyond, upon reaching the road, turn left and cross over to the opposite side and in a few yards the Queens Head will be on your right. Walk on (you may want to call there of course!) and at the village store, turn right into Church Street. St Mary's church will be there almost immediately. What tales are locked up in the Old School House . . . sadly the building no longer serves that function. We noted that the 16th-century building called Hob Johns had a modern namesake, Hob Jons.

The area to the left at the bottom of Church Street was the site of the old village pond – can't you just imagine the heavy horses being watered there!

SLINFOLD

Length : 5¼ miles

Getting there: Slinfold village lies approximately 5 miles west of Horsham. If approaching on the A29, turn east 2 miles north of Five Oaks, about 8 miles south of Ockley.	Parking: There may be space in Clapgate Lane on the west aspect of the church. An alternative is to use the Kings Head car park, if you are patronising the pub.	Maps: OS Landranger 187, Dorking, Reigate and Crawley area; Pathfinder, Horsham and Cranleigh. Starting point GR: 117316.

Lying close to the A29, Slinfold's apparent remoteness is remarkable. It is a widely dispersed village, although the majority of its old houses and cottages form a tight concentration around the village shop, the pub and St Peter's, one of the better examples of Victorian church restorations.

The walk starts from Clapgate Lane, a thought provoking name. A lane undoubtedly used by heavy horse teams with the gates along its length almost certainly being triggered by simple devices to open and close them.

The route passes Hill House, a massive

FOOD and DRINK

The village has one pub, the Kings Head, a handsome old building, thought to be of early 1600s vintage, directly opposite the general store and post office. It is open seven days a week, serving bar meals, sandwiches and ploughman's on Tuesday to Saturday and at lunchtime on Sunday, snacks only on Mondays. There is a play room as well as an extensive garden, and a children's menu is offered on Monday to Saturday. Telephone: 01403 790339.

---

establishment dominating the whole immediate area, and extends into open and undulating Wealden farmland. Beyond Rapkyns, a large house now used by the NHS, is Rapkyns Farm. At the end of the walk you can either return to your car by way of the church and churchyard or explore the east side of the village – or both.

THE WALK
❶ Walk northwards up Clapgate Lane and in only a short way you will pass by a cluster of old houses and Clapgate Cottage just beyond. With a three-way sign on the left continue straight on through a gateway then shortly Hill House will come into view on the left. With a two-way sign in front of you, turn right into the footpath and no doubt you have paused to get another view of Hill House down its driveway. You are quite high above a ghyll (ravine) on the left and the well-made path continues down through woodland. With a two-way sign on the left you join a field path; the river Arun with hedges is on your left. On the high ground to your right is Rowfold Farm. You pass by, also on the left, a three-way sign. Walk on, still having the

hedge and river for company to a bridge. Go over it and turn right; as you do so there will be a gate and a three-way sign on the right.

❷ Your previous companions of hedge and river are now on your right. Walk on to the next corner of this field where, at the two-way sign, you turn left. Go up the rising ground and at the top turn right at the two-way sign, going through a wicket gate. Now on a wide grassy track you go through fenced paddocks and pass a three-way sign on the left, in which direction Nowhurst Farm is in full view. Beyond a gate, go onto a gravel path. There will be a two-way sign on the right and just beyond, close by a barn, turn right at the three-way sign, going through a wicket gate. This takes you into a short stretch of enclosed path. Then, going by a two-way sign on the right and bearing right, you head for a converted barn with a clock tower.

Bearing left, walk on towards the two-way sign and you have a choice of stile or gate to get into the next field. Now in the field, and with a hedge on the left, follow it around by the field path. In the corner at a gateway, go over the stile here and the next one, then, at the two-way sign, turn

---

PLACES of INTEREST

The tiny village of **Itchingfield**, remarkable for its lovely old church and well preserved Priest House, is to the south-east. Just beyond is **Christ's Hospital School** (the Blue Coat School) where the distinctive uniform is a long-skirted over garment and yellow stockings. The fascinating chapel is open to the public. For details of the Beating Retreat ceremony contact Horsham Tourist Office.

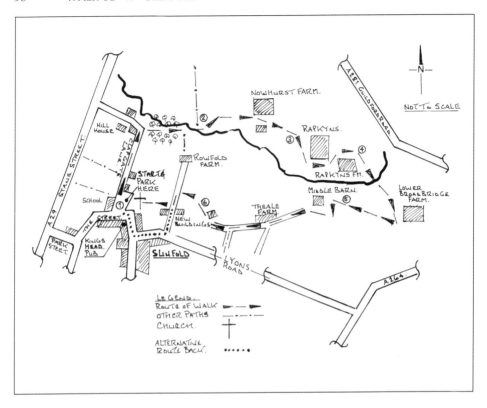

right to go over a makeshift 'bridge' across a ditch.

❸ You have come out into an obvious area of garden, but be assured, you are on the legal right of way. Now go through the wicket gate set in the fence and walk over to the two-way sign at the other gate across the field. Hopefully, you will be, as we were, greeted by two gentle donkeys. There is a small wood to your right in this pasture. Walk over to an oak tree, beyond which you go over two stiles either side of a track (Cooks Lane). There is a four-way sign here. Once over the second stile, bear right across this small field to go over a slatted 'bridge' and stile. The enclosed path then comes to a fence, and just beyond it, on the left, is a two-way sign. As you came down the previous path you will have caught sight of a large house. Continuing now, iron fencing will be on your left and Rapkyns, with its extensive grounds, will come clearly into view – how beautiful the landscaping is with the lake and specimen trees. The field path will follow closely the iron boundary fence. Then it continues into an area of brambles, but the way is quite clear and will lead to a two-way sign at a stile. Continue into this next field to follow the fence, still on your left. Over to your right is Rapkyns Farm where you can now see the examples of old restored barns.

Our donkey chums at Rapkyns

❹ Follow the path around by the fence to a three-way sign. Go over the stile here and turn right. Continue by the first entrance gates into Rapkyns Farm and just beyond the second entrance way turn right over the stile at the two-way sign. Go immediately left onto the field path and in only a short way turn right across this field at a two-way sign to head for the next waysign. Go over the stile there in the fence, with Rapkyns Farm and its various buildings to the right. Continue through the opposite gate at the two-way sign. Bearing slightly right, walk to the opposite corner of this field and there between two gates at a two-way sign, go over the slightly ramshackle stile. Then with a gate on your left, bear right into an enclosed path between fence and trees. Go over the next stile at a two-way sign on the right and, bearing slightly left into this pasture, walk towards the trees in front of you. There, in the fence, go over the stile at a two-way sign. This path leads to a railway sleeper bridge – please be careful, some sleepers are insecure. On the other side, and at a two-way sign on the right, turn right and follow the field path with the hedge and stream on your right. You will see the buildings of Lower Broadbridge Farm, through the trees in front of you. Coming then to a farm track junction, turn right across a 'bridge' over the river.

❺ Despite its lack of waysigns, this wide grassy farm track continues on its quite unmistakable route, giving views to the right of both Rapkyns and Rapkyns Farm. You then go over another bridge and eventually, with a mature oak tree in front of you and a house (Middle Barn) to its left, the track turns left and sharply right around the house. Just beyond its boundary fences on the right and bearing slightly left, the track goes across the next field where, on the right, is a twin track concrete driveway which serves Middle Barn. The roof tops and chimneys of your next landmark, Theale Farm, are in sight through the trees ahead.

The field path then joins the concrete trackway and leads, at last, to a two-way sign directing you through a wicket gate at a cattle grid. Theale Farm is now on your right. The route continues past the farm on the trackway. This leads to green painted gates, beyond which you continue on a stony farm track with trees on either side. Shortly past a three-way sign on the left, the track continues to a lane junction. With a three-way sign on the right, turn right. Go across the cattle grid and

through the wicket gate to the left of it. This takes you into a path alongside a house with a 'ham' radio mast. From the house, the field path continues down into a small wood and over two stone slab bridges, emerging then into a field. Turn right at the two-way sign; Slinfold church tower is now in sight across the field. Follow the field path to its next corner and there at the two-way sign, turn left.

❻   Continuing up the field path, New Buildings Farm is over to your left. You emerge onto a farm lane and there, with a three-way sign on the right, turn left. Coming then to New Buildings Farm and with a two-way sign on the right, you now have a choice. Option one is to continue straight on and join Lyons Road, turning right for The Street and returning through Slinfold village. Option two is to turn right at the waysign and continue on the path into the churchyard via a paved track, perhaps visiting the church en route to your car.

SHIPLEY AND DRAGONS GREEN
Length: 3¼ miles

Getting there: Approaching from the A24, turn west on the A272 at the Buck Barn cross-roads and garage, then turn south at the sign for Shipley. If using the A29, turn east at	Billingshurst onto the A272. Beyond Coolham, turn south where signposted. **Parking:** Park in the village car park in School Lane between	the windmill and the church. **Maps:** OS Landranger 198, Brighton and The Downs; Pathfinder, Billingshurst. Starting point GR: 144219.

The village of Shipley is very widely scattered and the few buildings you will see lie between the church and the windmill. In contrast, the hamlet ('a cluster of homes without a church') of Dragons Green is tightly concentrated, where else but in Dragons Lane.

Shipley's windmill is the biggest in Sussex, built in 1879 and now restored to full working order. It is open to the public at certain times in the summer – for details telephone 01403 730439. A magnificent sight when it's in operation, the whoosh of its sails is a sound you're not likely to

FOOD and DRINK

The George and Dragon started life as two farm cottages in the 16th century and is a delightful old place where you must 'duck and not grouse'; those beams are pretty hard. There is a very wide range of specials and the meals can only be classified as gargantuan, all prepared from fresh produce, individually cooked to order and well presented. Food is available seven days a week and at each session of lunch and dinner except Sunday evening. This pub has limited indoor eating accommodation and is very popular, therefore booking is a good idea. Telephone: 01403 741320. Outside there is a large garden and a children's play area. Shipley's only pub is the Countryman, in Countryman's Lane some way to the south-west of the village. It is a comfortable establishment offering good food.

forget. The mill was once owned, along with Kingsland, the nearby house, by Hilaire Belloc (1870–1954), the author and poet who immortalised Sussex in his writings.

The parish church, St Mary's, is Norman, built by the Knights Templars during the 12th century. Its size is an indication of the community it once served; the rural population up to and including the period between the Wars was huge compared to the present day.

Dragons Green with its attractive half-timbered cottages is as rural and isolated as its neighbour, despite the fact that both are relatively close to the A272. There is the popular belief that the hamlet saw the demise of the last dragon in England. If true, this would probably have been a monitor lizard – those in the Far East are dragon size!

Its pub, the George and Dragon, is unique in that I know of no other that has a grave headstone in its front garden. This remembers Walter Budd, the albino and epileptic son of the owners in the late 19th century, who was driven to suicide as a result of taunting. He was buried in the churchyard under the words 'May God forgive those who forgot their duty to him who was just and afflicted'. When the church authorities insisted that the headstone should be removed, the lad's parents, in an act of defiance, erected it in their garden. That was a brave act in those days, good for them!

THE WALK

❶ Leave the village car park by turning left onto School Lane and, with Kingsland then to your left, go right over the stile opposite at the waysign and large oak tree. Keep the hedge in this field on your right and go through a gap in the next hedge in front of you. There is usually a spring-loaded wire across the gap – please be sure to replace it behind you. Go over the next stile at the two-way sign, with Church Farm North over to your left, and, bearing slightly left, walk over to a three-way sign you will see on the other side. As you approach, you will see two fence posts close together; at the line of posts, go through these and over the bridge where only a few

PLACES of INTEREST

The Blue Idol (the name is explained if you go there), the Friends Meeting House where William Penn, 1644–1718, founder of Pennsylvania, had such an influence, can be found off the A272 west of Coolham. A lovely old, peaceful place, maintained in almost the same state as in Penn's time (GR: 108232).

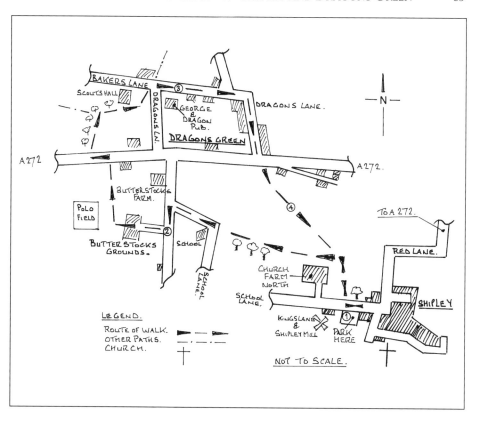

NOT TO SCALE.

yards further on to your right you go over another bridge and through two more posts. Go over the stile now opposite, continue up this field with its hedge on your left and, at the corner with a two-way sign, turn right and walk on to a single oak tree. Just beyond, turn left to go through a gateway. Make for a large oak tree, in fact one of three, directly in front of you. As you get to the third oak you will see a gate and waysign. Beyond it at the field boundary (using either the gate or stile) go out onto School Lane, turning right. Continue on by a waysign and track on the right and then at the junction of School Lane and Smithers Hill Lane, turn left.

❷ In only a few yards, turn right into the waymarked farm track, signposted 'Butterstocks Grounds'. You will come then to a gate leading into a stableyard. Walk onto a two-way sign in front of you and continue on the metalled lane. Go through the gateway into the field. Now bearing slightly left, walk over to the left-hand corner; an oak tree there will guide you. Coming to a two-way sign, go through the gate to turn right onto a chalk track. A polo field is on your left.

Then, with the track going off into the polo field, walk ahead on the grassy track with a two-way sign on the right, carrying on to a gateway and stile. There is a large barn-like building here on your right. Once beyond this at the junction with the A272 cross over and turn left. In only about 150 yards and coming to a waysign on the right, go over the two stiles there and turn left into the field. Walk on to its corner, with a two-way sign at a stile and gate. Here turn right to continue in the new direction in the same field, with a hedge and fence on your left. Across the field to your right you will see Oakleigh Farm House in its lovely grounds.

Just beyond a two-way sign on the left turn right at a three-way sign and go across the field to the next stile and waysign. In this next field, bear slightly left, going towards a waysign and gate. Go through into the next field and make for the hunt gate, stile and waysign. Go through the gate and turn left. Follow this field path with the hedge on your left. To your right, and tantalisingly close across the field, is the George and Dragon pub, but you're not there yet!

On the left you will go by a small wood and there in the next corner of the field, at the two-way sign, turn right and continue around on the field path. With a children's play area on the left just beyond the fence you will suddenly come upon the handsomely thatched building which is the 1st Shipley scout headquarters. There is a gate and waysign to the right of it. Go out onto Bakers Lane. Turn right and in only a few yards beyond you really have reached the pub.

❸ From the pub turn right into Dragons Lane. The first house on your right looks to be a modern building but was, as you will

see, built in 1903 – why then did the builder call it Korea Villas? What a picture book cottage is Yew Tree. Then at a double junction bear right, still on Dragons Lane, and yet another delightful cottage comes into view on the right. With a waysign and track on the left, keep on the lane. Having passed by Box Grove and its lovely garden on the right, you come to a building with a Victorian postbox set in its wall. At the junction leading to a modern crescent of houses there is a local produce stall. Next at the junction of the lane with the A272 cross straight over. With a three-way sign on the right, go over the stile at the gate into a field and, with its hedge close by on the left, continue up its rising ground. When you top the rise you have a splendid view of the Downs, and in the middle distance the buildings of Church Farm North. At the end of this long field path you go through an old gateway. Watch out for the spring-loaded wires across the path, and then, with a two-way sign on the left, join the wide farm track.

❹ At a track junction and two-way sign on the left, carry straight on. The buildings of the farm are now in clear view. You will then reach your outward route and at the three-way sign turn left to go through the familiar sets of posts and over the two bridges, making for the stile and waysign in the field corner – and what a delightful view you will get of Shipley Mill. Once over the stile you will, of course, be heading for the last one at the oak tree and, coming out onto School Lane opposite Kingsland, you turn left to the car park, with the church beyond.

WARNHAM AND ROWHOOK

Length: 1¾ or 6¾ miles

Getting there: Warnham lies to the north of Broadbridge Heath on the B2199, and is also directly signposted off the A24, north of Horsham. Rowhook is north-west of Horsham and is signposted off the A29 south of Oakwoodhill.

Parking: The village hall car park in Hollands Way, Warnham. If you want to start the walk in Rowhook, you can leave your car at the Chequers pub, where permission will be readily given, subject to the usual proviso.

Maps: OS Landranger 187, Dorking, Reigate and Crawley area; Pathfinder, Horsham and Cranleigh. Starting point GR: 157335 (Warnham), 122342 (Rowhook).

Both the longer and shorter routes of this beautiful Wealden walk take you through Warnham village via Friday Street and Church Street which contain the majority of its old houses and cottages, and thoroughly charming they are too. Field Place, just to the south, was the birthplace of Percy Bysshe Shelley (1792–1822), the poet. Unfortunately, there are no footpaths in its immediate area and the house is not open to the public.

The going is all over good dry tracks

FOOD and DRINK

The Greets Inn at Warnham is a lovely old pub, full of character. The food here is *par excellence*. Bar meals, sandwiches and the like are available and there are summer and winter menus. It is open seven days a week and food is served at all sessions, except Sunday evenings. Children are welcome in the delightful garden and the restaurant. Telephone: 01403 265047. In addition, there is another pub in the village, the Sussex Oak, just off the route of the walk.

The Chequers at Rowhook is of 15th-century vintage and was purpose built as a pub. Its exterior belies its delightful interior which retains a great deal of the original arrangement of its quaint old rooms. This house has good, cooked to order food, produced from fresh ingredients, and plenty of it. There is a garden with play facilities, and children can eat there or in the restaurant. The Chequers is open seven days a week and food is available at all sessions. Telephone: 01403 790480.

THE WALK

❶ From the north-east top corner of the Warnham village hall car park walk out by the large oak tree and bear left to make for a large chestnut on the west side of the field – it has a wide gap on one side of it in the hedge. This will bring you out at a road junction, Hollands Way and Lucas Road. Bear left into the latter and, coming to the junction with Tilletts Lane, cross straight over into the signposted path opposite. Once beyond the small woodland with a new housing development on the left, bear right across the field on the clearly defined path to its north-west corner. Turn left onto a wide farm track which continues with hedges and trees to the right, giving uninterrupted views across the Weald to the South Downs.

Going into the next field, with trees and hedges still on the right (then shortly going by a two-way sign on the same side), the track comes to an old gateway, stile, three-way sign and small pond on the right – walk on by these. You will already have another three-way sign in sight; here turn right through the gateway. You are, of course, still on the same wide farm track, the trees still with you on your right.

and paths with no hills, and the views are quite spectacular. For a short way at Rowhook the route is on that famous Roman road, Stane Street, which linked Chichester (Novio Magnus) to London (Londinium) Bridge. Yes, if you concentrate you can hear its traffic . . . well, we liked to think so! The former importance of Warnham is reflected in the size of its parish church, St Margaret's (formerly St Mary's), certainly well worth worth a visit.

Starting at Warnham, you can either choose the full circuit through Rowhook then south to the river Arun, or the 1¼ mile walk into the woods to the west of the village. Another option is to leave your car at Rowhook and pick up the directions south through Townhouse Copse.

PLACES of INTEREST

Horsham, to the south, has a modern town centre where Swan Walk contains a memorial to Warnham's Shelley. Not far away is the old area around the parish church, St Mary's. It really is a delight, full of old listed buildings which have been well preserved.

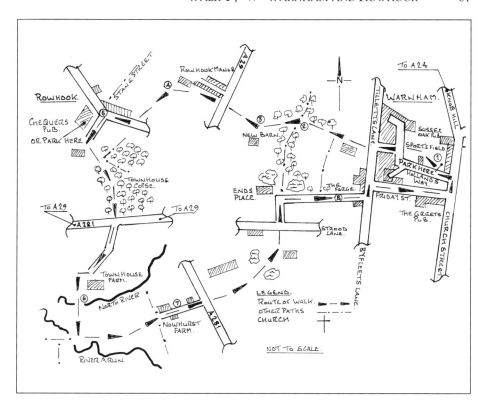

❷ The track goes into trees and in a few paces you reach a junction and four-way sign.

For the shorter walk, you turn left here into an enclosed track which will take you on down to the entrance gates to Ends Place. There at the three-way sign you turn left onto its drive or footway, to follow the directions back into Warnham as in the last paragraph below.

To continue on the longer route, keep the waysign on your right and turn right, going up a flight of steps over a stile into a field; you still have the views to the south. Now a fence and hedge will be on the right. The field path comes to a stile set in the fence and there are two oak trees on your left. Beyond this stile the way continues on a broad grassy track with trees, hedges and fence on your left. Next, at a gateway, stile and three-way sign, walk straight ahead across the next field on a clear path. The building you will see to your left is New Barn. About halfway across this field you will see ahead of you a two-way sign. Passing it on your right, you will once again be on a broad grassy track heading towards a wood. Ignoring then a track going off to the right, go down to, and cross over, a substantial footbridge taking you into another field, on the other side of which make for the two-way sign just beyond a single oak tree.

Farlington School, Rowhook

❸ Now the path continues with a ditch and hedge on your left and New Barn still in sight on the same side. Coming then to a gateway, stile and two-way sign, walk across this field to the gate, stile and waysign on the far side. Over to your right you will see Rowhook Manor and to the left a large area of farm buildings. Go over the stile which brings you out onto the verge of the busy A29 road (make sure you can cross it safely). Go over the opposite stile at its gateway and waysign. You follow a hedge on your right for a few yards to a stone wall where you bear left onto a paved path; Rowhook Manor is now on your right. This paved path will take you through a pergola (yes, this is the legal right of way). Then with a tennis court on

your left and bearing right, you will come to a fence with a stile at a gate. The path continues on beyond, with a fence and initially some buildings on your right, then some mature oak trees. Go over the stile at the next fence – a slightly unorthodox one!

❹ Now, in this new field and with a line of trees at its next boundary in front of you, head for the distinctive gap where you will also see a timber powerline pole. Just beyond (with a two-way sign to your right, and here bearing right towards trees in front of you) be vigilant as you have to locate a narrow gap in those trees. Between one oak tree on the right, with another just beyond it on the left (with a two-way sign), turn left onto a broad grassy track and, keeping the trees on your left, further on and on the same side, you will see buildings through the trees. This field then converges into a corner confined by two hedges and there you go over a stile. The buildings on your left are now close at hand and in this small field, with a fence on the right, you will be heading for Rowhook Farm. Go over the next stile to bear left at the garden fence into a wire-enclosed path, at the top of which, at a waysign, turn right onto Rowhook Road with Stane Street Cottages on your right. You are now heading for the Chequers at Rowhook which still has the hamlet's stocks in its front area. Turn left at the lane junction.

❺ *If you are starting the walk from Rowhook, follow the directions from this point.* With the pub on your right and its car parks beyond, continue along the lane (the route of Stane Street). At the entrance way to Northern Lights on the left, at the waysign there, turn left, going up some steps. The fenced path directs you to turn right at a two-way sign bringing you out into a field. Make for the buildings on the far side of it, aiming to arrive with the farmhouse on your right. This will bring you to a waysign in the field corner. Go over the stile there, taking you at first into the garden of the house on your right, then over another stile where, at the three-way sign on the left at a footbridge, you bear right into the woodland of Townhouse Copse. The path will at all times be on the fringe of the wood and have a fence on the right with open ground beyond. Along the ½ mile stretch of this path you will meet some obstructions but the course of it is clear on the ground. The fence should always be close by on the right.

You will finally emerge on the north verge of the A29 (please take care). Turn right, then left into the signposted Town-house Farm track, then in a few hundred yards you will come to the farm and its entrance way and cattle grid – watching out that you don't fall over the pheasants! Turn right, then left at the two-way sign into a field. The farm, its buildings and garden will be on your left. Then, with another two-way sign on the right, follow the field path and once beyond the fences of the property the path passes several large oak trees on the left as you head for a wood.

❻ The clear path takes you into the wood and over the footbridge across North River, into open country. With Rowfold Farm on the skyline to the right, the path once again goes by oak trees, but now on the right. At the end of this field path, with a gate in front of you, a footbridge to the right of it and a three-way sign, turn left to follow the path along the line of the hedge on the right. At the two-way sign in the field corner, turn left.

At the top of the rise in this field, at a two-way sign on the right, turn right through a wicket gate onto a wide grassy track with horse paddocks on either hand. With a gate stile and three-way sign on the left, and Nowhurst Farm well in sight, continue to the end of this track. At its gate (which you can bypass) walk ahead onto a stony track, with a two-way sign on the right and another three-way sign and wicket gate on the same side. Walk straight ahead. The farm buildings will be on your left and barns on the right, and you pass the farmhouse on the left.

❼ Continue to the end of Nowhurst Lane and emerge onto the A281 by Strood Cottage. Cross over into the waysigned path almost directly opposite and, in a few paces, go over a stile. The continuing path is enclosed by fences with open fields to the right and Farlington School to the left. Then, with a two-way sign on the left and another house on that same side (where, just beyond, this path ends at a two-way sign) bear left, making for a stile and two-way sign now in sight. Once over this stile and with a three-way sign on the left, bear right and the fenced path will take you by a large lake to the right. This leads to a track going between hedges.

A little further on you will see the buildings of Strood Park Farm to your left. Coming to a crossing track with a three-way sign on the left, turn left, then almost immediately right onto a short stretch of woodland track. This brings you out onto a driveway to a house on the right with a two-way sign on the same side. Go straight across the driveway to emerge onto Strood Lane, with a waysign on the left. Bear right on the road and turn almost immediately left at the waysign onto the gravel entrance into South Lodge. Walk on into the continuing track beyond, which will take you up to a four-way sign.

Walk on a few paces to a two-way sign beyond and this will reveal the large red-brick building of Ends Place. Turn right onto the footway. Passing a two-way sign on the right and coming to Ends Place entrance gates, use the wicket gate to go out onto the continuing footway or the metalled driveway beyond.

❽ Continue on the full length of the drive or its footway. Then, with Fleetwood Lodge on the right, bear left into the approach way of The Forge and there, at the two-way sign, take the short section of footpath coming out onto Warnham's Byfleets Lane. Turn left. At the junction of Tilletts Lane and Friday Street, turn right into the latter to shortly have the Greets Inn on your right. All that remains now, of course, is a quiet wander up the street, turning left into Church Street, left again into Hollands Way and back to the village hall car park either to finish your walk there or return to Rowhook, following the directions in paragraphs 1 to 4 above.

RUSPER

Length : 2¾ miles

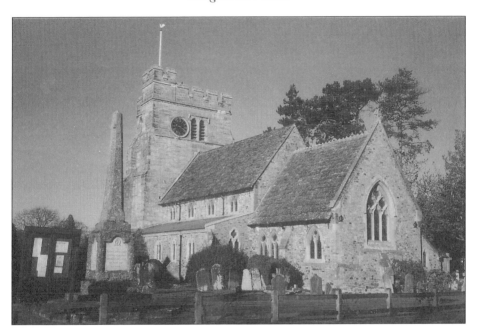

Getting there: Rusper lies about 5 miles north of Horsham. Coming from the north on the A24, turn off at Beare Green and reach the village through Newdigate. Coming from the south on the A24, turn off at Warnham to take the sign-posted road to Rusper.

Parking: There is a very convenient parish council car park next door to the church on its north side. Alternatively, patrons of the Star can use its car park.

Maps: OS Landranger 187, Dorking, Reigate and Crawley area; Pathfinders, Horsham and Cranleigh, and Crawley. Starting point GR: 205374.

This is a truly 'border village'. Only a few yards from the car park from where this walk starts is the Sussex Border Path and you are almost in Surrey. Just north of the Plough Inn in Rusper's High Street is Ghyll Cottage, which is itself a neighbour to Ghyll Manor. The word 'ghyll' is a Norse one used to describe a water-cut ravine and here at Rusper is one of the finest examples in the county of that phenomenon. In fact, you will walk above it for about the first ¾ mile on the Border Path and at one point descend almost to the level of the stream at its bottom. You will be enclosed along this path by the lovely Horsegills Wood, thickly carpeted with bluebells in springtime. The return is thoroughly rural and will bring you to the southern end of Rusper which has many treats to offer in its attractive old houses and cottages. A feature of this village is that the school bell is rung every day at 9 am to give pupils notice of where they ought to be, as opposed to where they might wish to be! Equally interesting is the restored pump outside the Star and opposite the store, and the church of St Mary Magdalene, dating from 1287, is well worth a visit.

THE WALK

❶ From the parish council car park go back out to turn left into the paved footway, initially going between a fence and hedge. Coming to the sports field, turn left onto it at the Sussex Border Path waysign on the right. Keep the hedge close by on your left. The path continues down

between trees to a stile and two-way sign leading beyond into a large field over which the course of the path is quite clear, heading for trees on its far side. You will pass by some isolated trees in the field on your left. From this point you will see a gate, stile and waysign at the field boundary. Continue, still on the Sussex Border Path (SBP), on the track through Horsegills Wood, with the deep ghyll on your right. In a few hundred yards and coming to a SBP waysign on the left, turn sharply right and here you will need to take care as the path descends very steeply down into the ghyll itself. On the way down there is a division of paths. You take the right-hand one, down to a footbridge.

❷ Once over the bridge, the path leads away from it up a series of steps. The track takes you on to a two-way sign on the left. Turn right to go over a stile at another two-way sign. Here you turn left into a very large field and continue on the path with the wood close by on the left. Coming to the corner boundary of this field, go over the stile at the two-way sign and you will be back in the woods. The ghyll is now on your left and you cross over it by a footbridge. Continue on the woodland path, which now follows the stream, and shortly you will cross over a third footbridge, taking you on to a SBP sign on

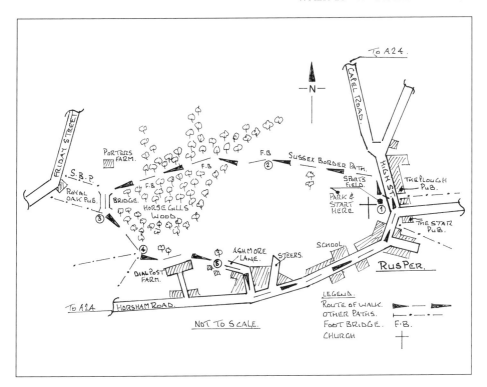

the left. Turn left to go over a bridge leading through a gateway into a field beyond; a two-way sign will be in the hedge on your left.

❸ Turn left onto the broad grassy farm track, with the wood on your left and lovely open countryside to your right. At the next field boundary, the farm track continues through a gateway. The farm track takes you on by a gateway on the left to a four-way sign at the corner of the wood.

❹ With the sign on your right, go on for a few paces and bear left off the farm track, walking through an old gateway. Bear right into the field, which has a group of isolated trees. Keep the boundary fence to your right and walk on towards the farm buildings, also on your right. As you leave the last of them, you go through a gateway at a two-way sign on the left, into the next field. Walk across the field, making for an oak tree with a timber power-line pole to its left, very close to some houses. Go on beyond the oak and there, in a garden hedge is a waysign. This brings you to a stile – go over it and bear left.

❺ Walk on down Ashmore Lane to meet Horsham Road where you turn left onto the footway and pass Steers, then the school, to return to your car.

BOLNEY

Length : 6½ miles

Getting there: The east/west approach is made on the A272 road. If using the A23, come off at the new interchange at Bolney and the road into the village is then a short way west. From the A24 turn east on the A272 at Buck Barn crossroads. Bolney village is signposted to the north about 3 miles east of Cowfold.

Parking: There is a village car park just north of the pub, or parking on the road is usually possible, but please not outside the general store and post office. In addition, permission can be obtained to park at the Eight Bells, with the usual proviso.

Maps: OS Landranger 198, Brighton and The Downs; Pathfinder, Haywards Heath and Cuckfield. Starting point GR: 261226.

Bolney village was formerly concentrated in two small areas, its few houses and cottages and shop adjacent to the church and pub, and a later section about ¼ mile further north, which contained quite a number of businesses, butcher, baker, a large general store (combining iron-mongery, agricultural supplies and general carriers to the whole area), all now gone. As you return down Bolney Street you will

FOOD and DRINK

The Eight Bells (its name coming from the bells in the neighbouring church) is a snug and comfortable pub serving a wide variety of food seven days a week, at lunchtime and in the evenings. Children are permitted in the garden or restaurant and half portions are available. Telephone: 01444 881396.

---

see that the shopfronts of both the baker's and butcher's shops are still in place. The area between the two parts of the village has, of course, been filled with modern houses.

Our walk soon reaches Bookers Farm, now a vineyard with a shop and they are happy to show people around. You continue by several more farms, a mixture of open and wooded countryside and then the quite spectacular approach to Rout Farm, sitting on its own high point on the Downs. The return route is through Wykehurst Park to the north end of Bolney and, after what we hope you will agree has been a lovely and varied walk, a visit to the lovely church is highly recommended. St Mary Magdalen is huge, reflecting, of course, the size of the community it formerly served, and contains many treasures. Possibly its most outstanding feature is its lychgate – the most massive and impressive of any we know in Sussex.

THE WALK

❶ Walk north up Bolney Street. This will bring you to the sports ground and telephone kiosk, both on the right. In a few yards, beyond the kiosk and immediately before the house called Leecroft on the left, turn left into the waysigned path (this sign

may be hidden in the hedge – but it is there). The path continues initially between houses and goes over a plank bridge, then into more open country. It is enclosed by fences but, having passed a pole barrier, it eventually exits onto Foxhole Lane. Here you turn left and almost immediately right into the signposted farm track going by Bookers Farm; its vineyards and buildings will be on your right.

❷ The track then goes through the entrance gates leading to the farmhouse and there, at a three-way sign on the left, turn right. You continue through farm buildings on either hand. In a very short distance you will come to a gate, stile and two-way sign. Your route continues by turning left onto the field path here. A hedge is directly on your left and you head towards (and pass under) main grid power-lines. Coming then to a stile and two-way sign, continue beyond into a small wood. Going down a flight of steps, the path leads on to a three-way sign; turn left to go over a footbridge. You then come out into open ground with a small orchard on your right. As you continue, the buildings of Old Mill House Farm appear on the left. Coming to a split rail fence, go over the stile. The path continues by the buildings between fences.

PLACES of INTEREST

A few miles to the north of Bolney and very easily reached by either the A23 or B2114 roads is **Nymans**, the huge National Trust property just to the south of Handcross, which, in addition to its nationally acclaimed gardens and grounds, has extensive woodland walks.

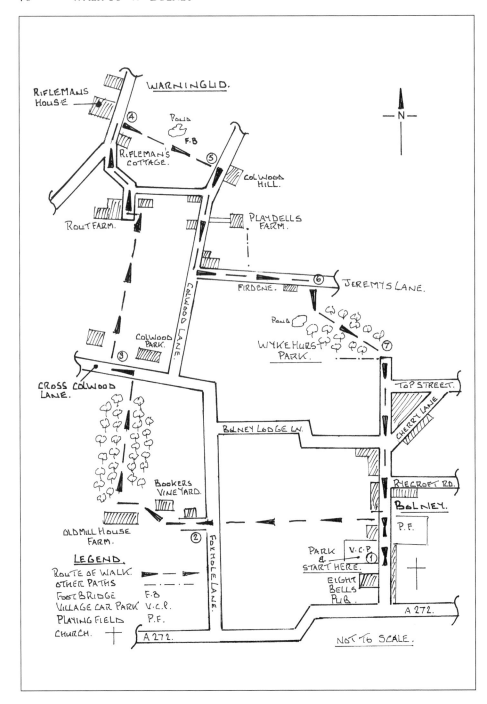

Go over the next stile to turn left. You will see a three-way sign at the track junction; now turn right into the enclosed High Weald Track. This gently climbing path, with woods on either hand, at one stage passes fruit orchards on the right. You continue through the woods, coming eventually to a gate and stile, beyond which the path goes over a small pasture containing mature oak trees. The clearly defined path goes over to a stile which takes you into Cross Colwood Lane. Turn left. The entrance way to Colwood Park and its lodge house are now on your right.

❸ Go on beyond the entrance way to Fig Tree Cottage on the right. Walk on then with a 'letters only' postbox on the left, turning right into the waymarked path, also signposted to Overhill and Little Grove. This path takes you to a two-way sign where you bear left and the broad, rising, grassy track now goes by Overhill House on the left, with open ground to the right. Beyond the house, the track levels out, giving good views to your left. Coming to a junction of tracks and going through more orchards, and still gently rising, the path reaches a line of trees, oaks and poplars. The right of way continues with the trees on the right and a fence on the left. At the top of this path, at a two-way sign, go through the wicket gate. Rout Farm lies directly ahead of you on its hill. Bear right onto the broad grassy track and follow this, keeping close company with the boundary fence on the right. Follow this up to the farm buildings and there, at a barn, go through a wicket at a two-way sign. Go straight across this field towards a gate, two-way sign and ramshackle stile.

Go over the stile and turn left into the farmyards. Through the yard gates and with a two-way sign on the left, turn right through the next gates. You continue on the paved farm track.

❹ With a two-way sign on the left, the farm track turns right. You continue through the gates in front of you and descend quite steeply to buildings at the bottom. In wet weather you will have to negotiate the ford here – it can be fun! The track, of course, starts to rise and opens up the parkland and house on the left. You pass a two-way sign on the right and approach other buildings. Go through a gateway. Rifleman's Cottage is on your right; the building to the front, now a private house, was the Rifleman's Arms pub. Just past the cottage, turn right at its garage. This path will go down to a stile and waysign by the east end of the building, taking you into a field. Keep the hedge close by on the left and, at the field boundary, go over the stile. The field path continues to this next field's boundary hedge. There, at the two-way sign, change direction as indicated by the fingerboard and you will be heading for a wide gap in the trees in front of you, to the left of which, as you get nearer, is a large pond. You will have to get up onto the higher level of its grassy bank, taking you to a plank bridge. From this point the path continues obliquely left across the field to its opposite corner. As you draw closer you will see the waysign at a double stile taking you into the field beyond.

❺ The direction of the fingerpost is correct and you should follow it up the rising ground of this field. Topping the rise, a building will be directly in front of you on the other side of the field, where there is a waysign, gate and stile taking you out onto Colwood Lane; as you see, the building was Colwood Hill. Turn right onto this very pleasant lane where you continue past the entrance way into Playdells Farm on the left and a short way beyond at the three-way lane junction you turn left into Jeremy's Lane (such names always prompt me to say, 'who, I wonder, was Jeremy?'). Pass by, on the right, the entrance way into Tower Cottage, so named because of nearby Warninglid Water Tower – and what a lovely view to the Downs through the entrance of North Cottage.

❻ Then at the entrance way to Firdene, on the right, there are two lamp standards marking the drive. Go over the stile there at the waysign and, with both directly behind you, walk on down the field to bring trees, surrounding a pond, on your right and trees also on your left. A lovely stretch of greensward. You will pass by a sheep shelter on your right. The path continues towards trees in front of you and, at the two-way sign, go over the stile, coming out onto a farm track. Bear right. In only a few paces turn left, taking the clearly defined path into the woodland (you are now in Wykehurst Park) leading to a stile set at a fence. Here you turn left and, with the fence directly to your right, follow the short section of path around to the next two-way sign, on your left, and

stile, on the right. Bear left and follow the well-defined path going through an area of scrub woods.

❼ Coming to a crossing track, walk straight ahead. Go by a two-way sign on the left and shortly beyond another, on the same side, you will be passing under the main grid powerlines with a pylon tower on your left. Then, with a two-way sign also on the left, bear right into the continuing track – blink and you may miss the next three-way sign and stile, also on the left. Carry straight on. The track will take you to a waysign and kissing-gate on the right – still walk straight ahead. This lovely old cart track continues under a road bridge, then buildings start to appear on the left. The track comes to a gate; go through its side wicket to come out at the junction of lanes at the top (north) end of Bolney village. You pass by some grand old buildings, including the Women's Institute, its plaque quoting 1881, and Southdown House, part of the general merchant's and hardware store. There can be few places that have taken so much care of their war memorial – it really is a lovely setting, a credit to the village. But not to be outdone and on the right is the charming Old Bakery and its neighbour, Bakehouse Cottage. Now all that remains is a wander down Bolney Street and perhaps to contemplate calling at Bookers Farm Vineyard shop again . . . last year, 1996, was, we were told, a very good year!

TWINEHAM AND WINEHAM

Length : 4¼ miles

Getting there: Twineham, not to be confused with Twineham Green, which is a short way to the north of it, lies west of Burgess Hill. Coming west or east, approach on the A272 and turn south, to the west of Bolney, signposted to Twine- ham at Crosspost. Alternatively, using the A23, turn off west ½ mile north of the Hickstead Showground, signposted to Wineham.

Parking: Leave your car in the lane leading off Twineham Lane, signposted to the parish church and school.

Maps: OS Landranger 198, Brighton and The Downs; Pathfinders, Haywards Heath and Cuckfield, and Burgess Hill. Starting point GR: 254199.

This walk starts from and returns to the parish church of St Peter at Twineham and you simply must visit this beautiful old building, which dates from 1516, replacing the earlier one of about the year 1291. It is an extremely rare structure, not only for Sussex but in the British Isles, as it is brick built and now wonderfully mellowed. The churchyard itself has a rarity, it contains a large plot (just inside the entrance gate) acquired by the Society of Friends (Quakers) in 1694 as a burial ground.

FOOD and DRINK

I promised one more rarity and this is it . . . the Royal Oak pub at Wineham. Photographic records show that nothing has changed here in the last 60 years; it really is a warm, living museum, with its stone and timber flooring, lovely fireplace, old furniture, no gambling or music machines (heaven in itself!). The only food available here is a wide choice of sandwiches, plain or toasted, ploughman's and, in the winter, soup. The pub is open seven days a week for both food and drink and has the added attraction of being a morris dancing venue. Telephone: 01444 881252.

However, this will not be the only rarity in store for you on this walk.

On this route Twineham's old buildings are represented by the church, the old Rectory close by and parts of the school. You start off via Twineham Place, a large dairy farm where you will have to negotiate the cow and barn yards – and all that implies! However, you are soon past it and into the lovely rural countryside beyond. After passing through the hamlet of Wineham, your journey continues past Grovelands Farm and Twineham Grange, on across the fields and over the river Adur, back to Twineham church.

THE WALK

❶ Leaving Twineham church car parking area, having the church on your right, walk into the waysigned path which leads to a ramshackle gate. Go over the stile at a three-way sign onto the field path beyond, keeping the hedge on your left. Then at the hedge corner, with a two-way sign on the left, head obliquely across the field towards the buildings of Twineham Place farm. As you come to the boundary fence on your

left you reach what I can only describe as a 'uniquely' constructed stile – with any luck the (Sussex) wire and pole gate will be open and you will be able to bypass it!. Beyond it you will be in the farm's yards with a two-way sign on your left. As you turn left onto the concrete farm track, the barns will be on your right, as will the farmhouse. Just beyond, go through a pair of iron gates to continue on the concrete track.

❷ Come to a stream bridge and a few paces beyond, at a two-way sign on the left, you turn right to go over a stile. With the pylon on your right go through a gap in the hedge just beyond. Once in this field bear over to the hedge, now on your left. This will bring you to a two-way sign; go over the stile in the hedge. The path takes you to a three-way sign. Go through the iron wicket gate and turn right. With a fence and hedge on your right you approach a substantial oak tree. A large house and farm buildings are on your left, Great Wapses Farm – and what an impressive farmhouse. Why, we wondered, did its frontage face north? Beyond the oak tree go through the gate and turn left, bringing you to a gate and three-way sign. (Note: this path has been re-routed and the arm of the waysign directing you obliquely across the field is no longer correct.) With the gate, waysign and hedge on your left, you must

PLACES of INTEREST

A close neighbour of Twineham to the east is **Hickstead**, the 'All England Horse Jumping Ground', in fact Hickstead Lane going east just north of the church will take you to it. The events here are publicised nationally.

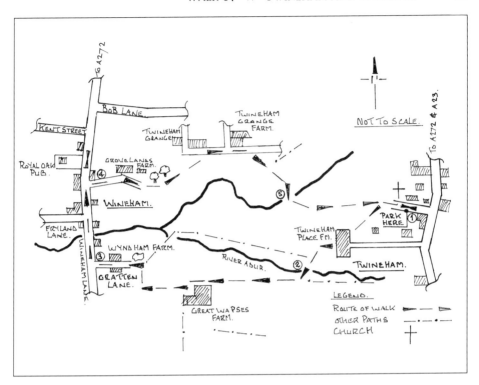

now walk around the headlands (the field's edges) which will then bring you to a three-way sign. (Note: all three arms on this waysign are pointing in their respective CORRECT directions.) Turn left through the gate onto a wide farm track lined with trees; this is Gratten Lane. Just beyond Wyndham Farm's large pond, on the right, go through the gate and out onto the gravel drive, then past the frontage of the farmhouse and down to Wineham Lane. Turn right.

❸ The lane continues over the river Adur and past the junction of Fryland Lane and a group of old houses. You continue up through Wineham hamlet, and very pleasant it is too. A little further up

Wineham Lane you come to Grovelands Lodge on the right and the drive leading to Grovelands. Next, on the right, is a house called Gatefield at the mouth of a farm track marked by a waysign. (Note: if you do not want to continue the short distance up to the pub you can turn right here and pick up the directions at point 4.) Reaching a house called Russets on the left, you then get the first sign of the Royal Oak pub ahead – how glad you'll be, I'm sure, that you decided to carry on to it.

❹ Coming out from the pub, turn right and walk back down to Gatefield, turning left into the waysigned farm track to reach Grovelands Farm and barns on the left. Bear right at the two-way sign on the right.

The Royal Oak at Wineham

The wide farm track will then continue out by two large oak trees on the left. Here you bear right, across open fields, then to a junction with another track, with a two-way sign facing you. Turn left. This takes you to a metalled farm track where, at a two-way sign, you turn right. A short way beyond Twineham Grange Farm, now largely an industrial site, with a pylon in front, turn right at the three-way sign into a rough field path. With a pylon on your left, the path goes directly beneath the powerlines. At a three-way sign, go over two plank bridges. Turn left beyond the second one, with a two-way sign on the right. A short way along this field path turn left at a two-way sign and cross another plank bridge and stile.

❺ You are now in a narrow but rough field and you make for the footbridge across the river Adur. Beyond the wicket gate on the other side of the bridge, with a two-way sign on the left, bear left, continuing between the hedge and pylon. With the pylon directly then to your right, turn left at the two-way sign. Keeping the hedge on your left, Twineham Place is over to your right. Coming to an iron field gate, go through its wicket and here, with a two-way sign on the left, bear left, but still with the hedge on the same side, into the next field. Next you will come to a weird Y-shaped stile – obviously related to the one you passed by (or over) earlier. Walk on across this field to the gate in its corner and go over the stile to rejoin your car.

ARDINGLY

Length : 7¼ miles

Getting there: Ardingly, north of Haywards Heath, is reached by taking the B2028 off the A272. The B2028 can also be taken southwards off the A264, east of Crawley. Once in Ardingly village turn off into Street Lane.

Parking: There are several options for parking in this village, including a free car park adjacent to the British Legion Club, accessible from Street Lane only, and on-road parking along the length of Street Lane. Permission to use the car park of the Oak Inn will be readily given, subject to the usual proviso. The walk starts and finishes here.

Note: The South of England Show takes place in Ardingly during the first week of June every year and the village gets very busy.

Maps: OS Landranger 187, Dorking, Reigate and Crawley area; Pathfinders, Haywards Heath and Cuckfield, and Crawley. Starting point GR: 342298.

The longest walk in this book, its objective was to circumnavigate Ardingly Reservoir and, as far as the various tracks and footpaths allow, that objective is achieved. It is necessary to walk (for about a mile) on the road up to Balcombe, but we have found it not to be overly busy even during the August holiday season. In any event this is a very small price to pay to be able to complete such a rewarding and interesting walk. It starts from the old part of the village, going by its very ancient church, St Peter's, and on down to the reservoir, where the on-going paths lead up to two magnificent buildings – Balcombe Place and Stone Hall – on the approach to which you will get wonderful views across to Balcombe railway viaduct, a splendid example of Victorian railway engineering for which a canal was cut to transport the bricks.

From Stone Hall you go out onto the

road and up to Balcombe where, from its southern outskirts, a footpath takes you across to Balcombe Mill – sadly no longer working. You will return on the reservoir's eastern path back to Ardingly. If you have binoculars do take them on this walk, wildfowl and waders abound on this large area of water. We were lucky enough to identify little egrets amongst the species we saw.

The going is over good, firm tracks, with one very short, steep hill just before the walk ends.

THE WALK

❶ From wherever you have decided to park start from the Oak Inn and continue westwards down Street Lane. Most of the houses immediately beyond the pub date from the 1930s but have been, in the main, constructed with sympathetic materials which have 'aged' well. Very soon there will be two old cottages, stone-built of course, Cobwebs and Knowle, next door to an old farmstead now converted to private residences. Knowle figures largely as a place name hereabouts, emphasised by another Knowle, the house this time.

As you continue, an area of Ardingly Show Ground is immediately on your right. Then, with two delightful old houses on the left, Jordans and Nottingham Cott-

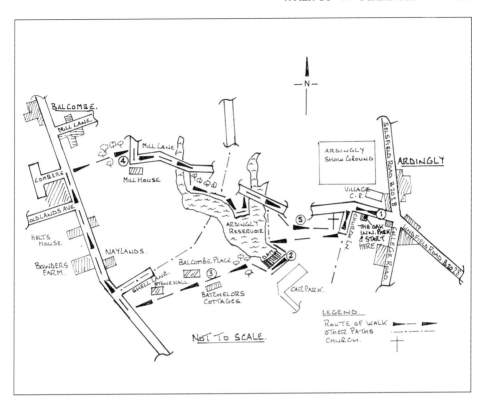

BALCOMBE.
MILL LANE.
COMBERS
MILL LANE
4
MILL HOUSE
OLDLANDS AVE
HOLTS HOUSE.
NAYLANDS.
BOWDERS FARM.
SHELL LANE
STONE HALL.
BALCOMBE PLACE
3
BATCHELORS COTTAGES.
ARDINGLY RESERVOIR
DAM
2
CAR PARK.
5
ARDINGLY SHOW GROUND
VILLAGE C.R.
ARDINGLY
SELSFIELD ROAD B.2028
1
THE OAK INN. PARK & START HERE
CHURCH LANE
COLLEGE ROAD
LINDFIELD ROAD B.2028
— N —
NOT TO SCALE.
LEGEND
ROUTE OF WALK
OTHER PATHS
CHURCH.

age, turn left into Church Lane with St Peter's church on your right, and what a lovely old building it is and quite unique, in our experience, for the large number of substantial tombs in the churchyard. The lane continues by large houses, secluded in their huge gardens, still with a predominance of Knowles. Coming to a two-way sign, bear right, then just beyond, at Town House Farm and with a waysign on your left, walk straight on into the field in front of you. Immediately part of the reservoir and the country beyond will be laid out before you.

❷ The course of the path going down this field is clearly defined and you will be heading towards a hedge in which you will see a gap. As you get closer, a two-way sign will come into view. Go through the old gateway there with its redundant stile, and you will, in this next field, be heading for another two-way sign. Upon reaching this sign you can use either the gate or stile to come out onto a sandy/stone track and here you have a choice of either turning left onto it (which will take you out onto the head of the dam wall) or as we did, with the gate behind you, walking down to the reservoir shoreline and bearing left around it (here is a bird watching hide). From here you mount the dam wall, turning right onto the sandy/stone dam head track which will take you to a pole gate.

Balcombe Place

With the Sailing Club building to your right, walk out onto the roadway. Down to your left is the extensive car park and picnic area. From the tarmac area, climb the bank in front of you, making for the four-way sign up on the raised level, and, with the sign on your right, walk towards the trees in front of you. On reaching the stile and two-way sign, go into this small wood where, in only a few yards at the next two-way sign, you go through the wicket gate. Walk up the rising ground and you will see the next two-way sign in front of you . . . what views there are!

Going through the gateway at the sign, bear over to your left. This will bring trees and a fence closer on your right and, continuing round by these, you will pass by a

two-way sign, also on your right. At about this point, and looking left, you will have a good view of Balcombe railway viaduct. Then, passing a double gateway on your right, a few paces further on, go over a stile.

❸ You are now in the parkland of Balcombe Place, the buildings of which are in view over to your right. To your left you will see a lovely old white-painted, half-timbered building, Batchelors Cottages. You change direction here and walk towards this house. Go through the gateway at the two-way sign and turn right onto a concrete farm track. Passing Batchelors Cottages on your left, the next landmark of Stone Hall will be ahead of you, with views still of Balcombe Place and yet another view of the viaduct to the left.

At the top of the concrete track, with a two-way sign, gateway and cattle grid on the right, turn left and, with Stone Hall Farm on the right, continue down to the Lodge House to turn right onto Stone Hall Lane (the Balcombe road), first passing the entrance into Stone Hall Farm and, beyond, the other entrance to Balcombe Place. Coming to Naylands and its Victorian postbox and waysign (to Nowhere!) all on the right, the road then goes by Bowders Farm. There will be other houses as you walk on heading for Balcombe, then you will be able to join a footway. You are, of course, now coming to the southern limits of Balcombe. At the road junction going into Combers Estate, and with a waysign approximately opposite, turn right through a gate into a field. (Note: at the time of walking this route, planning application had been lodged to develop a housing estate in this field, but if it comes about the pathway will still be signed.) The path now goes through another gateway and, once into this field, heads towards a powerline pole. On reaching the pole pass it by on your left. You will see the path continuing to other gates and waysigns. Coming to these, ignore the one on the left and its three-way sign; walk on the few paces to go through a single wicket gate.

❹ Here the path goes down a series of fairly steep steps bringing you to Mill Lane and opposite Mill House. Turn right and, just beyond, with The Mill on the right, go over the road bridge. With the lane climbing fairly steeply, walk on the 400 yards or so to turn right into the signposted sandy/stone track which will then follow the eastern side of the reservoir. At one point on the distant skyline, you will see the building of Ardingly College Chapel. At about this time you will pass by, on the right, a large bird watching hide. Having gone by a three-way sign on the left, the track eventually brings you out through a gate onto the causeway road across the neck of the reservoir. Turn right onto it and on the other side is the waysign, on your right, for the continuing track around the reservoir. However, you continue on the road to keep a sharp look out for the next waysign, which will be on your right and opposite to the entrance way into one of the satellites of Kew Botanical Gardens. Turn right, going down a flight of steps to cross a footbridge and then another and, with a two-way sign on the left, go just beyond it and turn left. A fence will then be on your left and for a short way the path climbs fairly steeply up through a pine wood.

❺ At the top, the path bears away to the left. On your right the extensive garden of a house is now in view. The path becomes enclosed and leads out at a two-way sign on the left, back into Church Lane. Turn left and very shortly you will be back at St Peter's church where you turn right into Street Lane to get a different aspect of the village as you approach it from this new direction.

WEST HOATHLY

Length : 2¾ miles

Getting there: West Hoathly lies to the north-east of Haywards Heath. From the A272 take the B2028 from Haywards Heath and turn off onto the minor road to Highbrook and West Hoathly. Alternatively, from the A264 Crawley/East Grinstead road turn south on the B2028 and about ¾ mile south of Selsfield Common turn east into the minor road signposted for West Hoathly and Sharpthorne.

Parking: Convenient for this walk and where permission is willingly given (with the usual proviso) is the car park of the Cat Inn at West Hoathly. Also, some on-street parking is usually available outside the church in North Lane.

Maps: OS Landranger 187, Dorking, Reigate and Crawley area; Pathfinder, Crawley. Starting point GR: 363326.

This walk starts from the footpath opposite the Cat Inn, going across lovely undulating Sussex North Weald countryside to the hamlet of Chiddinglye. The major feature here is the house of that name and its approach drive is through an avenue of Wellingtonia (California big tree, *Sequoiadendron giganteum*), the only such avenue lined with these huge trees that we know of and which you see to full advantage as you pass by the entrance.

From here the route turns south over farmland and through woods to come out at Philpots Manor school, one of 600 such schools world wide, based upon the philosophy and principles of Rudolf Steiner, philosopher and scientist (1861–1925).

The east-bound leg takes you back into West Hoathly via North Lane and what lovely old cottages and houses lie along its length, including the wonderfully preserved Priest House which is also the museum. (A phone call to 01342 810479 will secure a leaflet of opening dates and times for a visit which you should not miss.) Your walk up North Lane will end with the manor house on the left and opposite is the church. If you do nothing else in this village, we urge you to walk through its churchyard, and going down some stone steps and bearing right will lead you to a refuge with seats giving views

to the South Downs which we claim are amongst the finest in Sussex – and you can see the comings and goings of Bluebell Line traffic too!

THE WALK

❶ Take the footpath which leads west off North Lane and is opposite the pub, identified by a stile at a gateway with a concrete (East Sussex style) waymarker down on the ground. Then with Manor Cottage on your left, beyond which the path continues into dense bramble bushes (and beyond these a short area of clear ground), the path takes you over a stile at a gate in the left-hand corner. Now, with a hedge on the right, the open ground on the left gives marvellous views across the Mid Sussex Weald to the South Downs beyond.

❷ This field path, in close company with the hedge and trees on the right, will come to a two-way sign and stile between two gates. This takes you onto a farm track which, as you continue down, will bring the first sight of the California big trees at Chiddinglye into view. At the end of the farm track and coming to a gate and stile, you have the choice of either, but please secure the gate behind you if you use it. Then, shortly beyond, at a track junction and two-way sign on the right, continue straight ahead on the concrete paved lane.

PLACES of INTEREST

Wakehurst Place and Gardens (NT) lie south-west of West Hoathly, off the B2028. The grounds are under the guardianship of Kew Gardens and are a must to visit in any season.

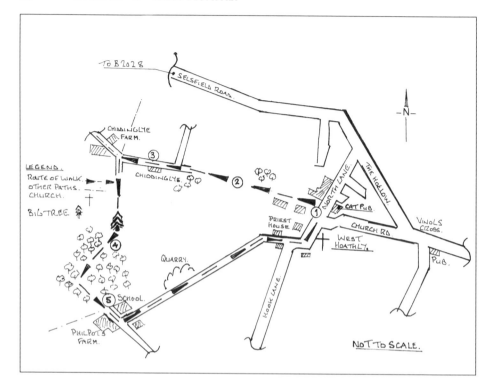

❸ This will take you by the entrance way leading to Chiddinglye Manor and, shortly beyond, at a four-way junction and three-way sign, Chiddinglye Farm will be to your front. Turn left and then at the point where the farm track bears right, go straight ahead and over two succeeding stiles. Once in the field beyond, make for the solitary California big tree at the far end. On reaching the redwood tree, turn around to get the view back to the house, its trees and farm. Leaving with the tree directly behind you, the field begins to narrow. Bear towards its left-hand corner and there to the left of two gates is a waysign – go over the stile there to enter a small wood.

❹   This path leads to a footbridge and then on to a 'squeeze gate' and another footbridge. Turn right at the waysign onto a field path with a hedge on the right leading to a two-way sign at a gate. Here turn left (not through the gate). The path now will take you to the opposite corner in this same field. There, go over a stile and almost immediately turn left at a three-way sign. You will now be in woodland and adjacent to a deep ghyll (ravine). Initially, this path will descend quite steeply and you need to watch your footing. Then, at the next two-way sign you go over a substantial footbridge. From this point on you may hear children's voices and the source will soon be revealed. The path then goes up a short series of stone steps. A play area of Philpots Manor school will be on your left. This path is strewn with tree roots – again, you should watch your footing.

❺ Coming to a crossing track and three-way sign on the right, turn left, bringing you out in the midst of the former buildings of Philpots Farm. Still bearing left, a two-way sign will be to your right and in a few yards, with another two-way sign on the same side, you take the left-hand track, going by some buildings belonging to the school.

Passing by the entrance way into the now disused Philpots Quarry (on the left)

this long lane, with its occasional views to the right, will bring you out at the junction of Hook and North Lanes, the latter being the southern area of West Hoathly village. You, of course, take this route and what a feast of lovely old buildings it has along its all too short length, amongst which is the Priest House, now in the possession of the Sussex Archaeological Society. But there are still gems to be revealed, including the imposing manor house opposite the church . . . but sadly you are at the end of this fascinating walk.

HORSTED KEYNES

Length : 3¾ miles

Getting there: From the B2028 which links the A272 with the A264 follow signs eastwards to Horsted Keynes between Haywards Heath and Ardingly. If coming southwards on the A22, branch onto the A275 and turn off west at Danehill.

Parking: You can either use the large free village car park adjacent to the post office and recreation ground, or the car park of the Crown Inn, if visiting the pub, or opt for on-street parking in Station Road near the Green Man pub.

Maps: OS Landranger 187, Dorking, Reigate and Crawley area; Pathfinder, Haywards Heath and Cuckfield. Starting point GR: 383282.

Horsted Keynes is just about as far east as you can get in West Sussex and, in fact, the Sussex Border Path almost (but not quite) splits this village, thus making it a good centre in this wonderful walks area in superb countryside. This is a very ancient place and it is of interest to note that the addition of Keynes (pronounced 'Canes') to Horsted indicates that it was 'awarded' after the Conquest, to the family of Cahances-Keynes who came from Caen in Normandy. This same family had many other possessions in Buckinghamshire, Devon, Dorset and Wiltshire and the villages in those counties also share the same suffix.

From the village green the walk goes into Church Lane, with its splendid concentration of old houses leading on to St Giles' church, such a lovely building. The route then goes out across the countryside to the west, over typical, gently undulating Sussex High Weald terrain. Then we come to the jewel in the crown of this walk . . . the Bluebell Line at Horsted Keynes railway station, where you may possibly have a dilemma. This is certainly not the place to rush by, with the comings and goings of frequent trains and the bustle of passengers and, of course, this could well whet your appetite for a 'real' train journey.

When eventually you do set off back, it is again over High Weald countryside but this time through more woodland and past large lakes until finally you join Church Lane once more.

Note: a vintage bus service runs from Horsted Keynes village to the railway station every Saturday. For details telephone 01825 723777.

THE WALK

❶ From close by the Green Man and on that same side take the path signposted 'to Church and School only'. At a fork in the lanes, turn right into Church Lane – a sign on the left will confirm your direction – and from here you will get your first view of St Giles' church at the other end of the lane. What a grand pair of gates at the approach to The Old Rectory. We wondered what the story was behind the middle cottage on the left whose name was Splinters!

At the church, with waysigns on the right, turn left onto the track signposted 'to St Giles School'; you cannot fail to appreciate the notice 'SLOW! FREE RANGE CHILDREN'. Reaching the school, with a three-way sign opposite, turn left into a stony path going through woodland and further on watch out as the path drops to a lower level. Shortly

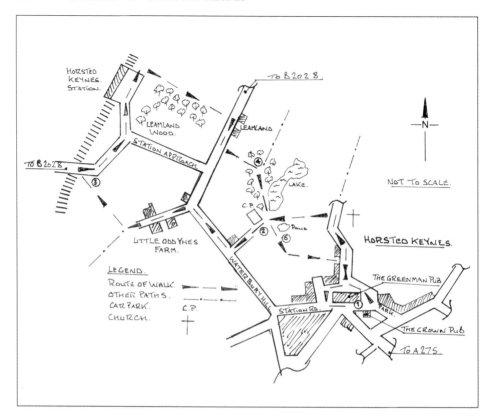

beyond you pass by, on the left, a lovely old half-timbered house and, with a two-way sign on your right, bear left into the continuing track and, although as yet you are still some way from the Bluebell Line, you may begin to hear the trains from this point.

❷ You now come to a large timber-framed barn which has been restored. There is an extensive lake on your right and then, with a four-way sign on the left, you walk straight ahead, passing by, on the right, a car park for the Isfield and District Angling Club. Coming then to a large corrugated iron barn, join the road (Waterbury Hill)

and turn right. In about 500 yards, and coming to a timber-clad house in front of you, turn left into the waymarked farm track. A Dutch barn comes into view ahead and you pass by a very handsome Georgian house on the right. Almost immediately you are in the barn yards of Little Oddynes Farm and, with a two-way sign on the right, you quickly come to a steel gate, which at first sight appears to be hinged at both ends! The top left-hand hinge has been incorporated as the locking device with a pin – be sure to secure it behind you. Only a few paces beyond and at a three-way sign, turn right through a small steel gate. Once in the field bear

Approaching the school at Horsted Keynes

slightly left towards the gate on the other side and, going through this gate, you will see your next two-way sign.

❸ As you get further across this field a bridge comes into view, part of the Bluebell Line. You will see the carriage works area through the trees to the right. Then, close to the bridge, go over the stile and turn right onto the road. Very soon, at the junction with Station Approach, bear left into the signposted roadway 'To Horsted Keynes Station' and there in a flash you are in another age!

When you are ready, in your own good time, leave the station and walk out to the picnic area beyond and, bearing left, follow the wide stone track, with a hedge and the railway line below on your left. Then at the top of the rise and coming to a sign 'No Through Road', turn right onto the continuing track to reach, in a few yards, a two-way sign. Go through the kissing-gate there into a narrow, enclosed path with Leamland Wood on your right and pass a gate leading into the wood on your right. There go over a stile at a two-way sign and almost immediately pass on the left another (redundant) stile and two-way sign and the fence-enclosed path then exits onto a road with the buildings of Leamland Barn opposite. Turn right on the road and in about 150 yards turn left over a stile at a waysign into a field. Keeping fairly close to the fence on your left in this field, walk on towards the visible waysign, going over the stile into Pains Wood. This woodland path will take you to a crossing track and there with a two-way sign on the right, continue your direction ahead.

❹ Go over a footbridge and then beyond it pass a two-way sign on the right. Once across two more footbridges you will see through the trees an expanse of water. Go over a series of footbridges at opposing angles to each other and then immediately beyond them and at a three-way sign on the right, turn right. The lake is now on your left. Coming to a crossways of tracks and a four-way sign in front of you and the

car park for the angling club on your right, walk into the opposite path, the waysign being on your right. This will bring you out onto a farm track, with a two-way sign on the left and gate on the right. Continue into the path ahead of you. Go through the next gate, or over the stile here, with a large pond on the left.

❺ You now have a lovely but different view of the old houses of Horsted Keynes in Church Lane. Go through two gates then turn right into Church Lane. On reaching the lane junction, go straight ahead and in a few paces and turning left you will come to the Green Man.